122

Down-to-Earth Ideas for Science Fiction Writers

122

Down-to-Earth
Ideas for
Science Fiction
Writers

Dave Haslett

ideas4writers

Other books in this series

Genre Fiction:

- 189 Seriously Good Ideas for **Comedy** Writers

- 215 Arrestingly Good Ideas for Writing Captivating **Crime** Stories

- 78 Brain-Stimulating Ideas for **Erotica** Writers

- 139 Practical and Imaginative Ideas for **Fantasy** Writers

- 92 Practical Ideas for Writing Authentic **Historical** Fiction

- 106 Frightfully Good Ideas for **Horror** Writers

- 87 Crafty, Compelling and Clued-up Ideas for **Mystery and Suspense** Writers

- 176 Lovingly Crafted Ideas for **Romance** Writers

- 122 Down-to-Earth Ideas for **Science Fiction** Writers

- 102 Powerful, Gripping and Intriguing ideas for **Thriller** Writers

The Elements of Fiction:

- 377 Ideas for Creating Memorable and Compelling **Characters**

- 94 Ideas for Writing Vivid and Evocative **Descriptions and Settings**

- 138 Ideas for Writing Dazzling and Authentic **Dialogue**

- 109 Ideas for Writing Better and More Dramatic **Plots**

- 81 Ideas for Adding **Strength and Structure** to Your Writing

- 21 Ideas for Identifying and Strengthening **Themes** in Your Writing

General Fiction:

- 394 Ideas for **Fiction** Writers: Create Unique, Compelling and Successful Stories Faster and Easier than Ever Before

- 192 Essential and Inspiring Ideas for Writing Bestselling **Novels**

- 87 Creativity-Boosting Ideas for Budding **Screenwriters**

- 65 Curtain-Raising Ideas for Writing Your First **Stage Play**

- 234 Easy Ideas for Successful **Short Stories** You Can Sell

- 125 Ready-to-Use **Storylines** to Instantly Inspire Writers

Practical Matters:

- 117 Painless, Efficient and Awesome Ideas for
  Editing and Strengthening Your Writing

- 218 Innovative and Inspiring Ways to Find Writing **Ideas**

- 128 Simple, Practical and Indispensable Ideas for
  Getting Your Writing Published

- 30 Confidence-Boosting Ideas for
  Overcoming Rejection and Getting Published

- 75 Money-Spinning Ideas for
  Self-Publishing and Marketing Your Writing

- 143 Smashing Ideas for Crushing Your **Writer's Block**

- 159 Creative and Inspiring **Ideas for Writers**

Children, YA, Nonfiction, Poetry, Travel:

- 201 Imaginative and Inspiring Ideas for **Children's Writers**

- 73 Creative and Inspiring Ideas for
  Young Adult/Teen Writers

- 301 Cut-Out-and-Keep Ideas for Writing **Magazine Articles**

- 160 Creative and Inspiring Ideas for **Nonfiction** Writers

- 125 Essential and Vers(e)atile Ideas for Writing **Poetry**

- 75 Worldly-Wise Ideas for **Travel** Writers

Introduction

Welcome, science fiction writers!

Within this book you'll find more than 122 powerful, down-to-Earth ideas to inspire stories, scenes, characters, situations, locations and more. We've even given you some instant, ready-made storylines that you can base your own scenes and stories on.

You'll also find plenty of insider tips and expert advice to help you improve your writing, write faster, get your work published, and much more.

You're welcome to use these ideas exactly as we've written them, or you can adapt them in any way that you wish. For example, you could use them as a starting point for your own ideas, and let your imagination wander. That could lead to your own cast of unique and individual characters, brand new stories, and all sorts of interesting and exotic locations to thrill your readers.

Although the ideas generally refer to the hero and villain as male, that needn't be the case. They would work equally well (or perhaps ever better) if either or both characters were female.

Don't forget to check out the other books in this series. We have tons of great ideas to help you improve your writing skills and craft, edit your work, sell and market it, overcome writer's block and rejection, find a publisher, or publish your books yourself, and much more.

The science fiction genre spans multiple sub-genres. If you're interested in writing steampunk or alternative history stories, for example, you'll definitely want to have a look at our collection of historical ideas. On the other hand, if sci-fi comedies are more your cup of tea, we have plenty of comedy ideas too. Or how about sci-fi fantasies? We have a terrific collection of fantasy ideas. Sci-fi romance? Or Sci-fi horror? We have collections for those too! And our collection of travel ideas might be just the thing if you want to set your stories in foreign lands.

The science fiction genre is huge and wonderfully versatile. You can combine the ideas in this book with those from any of the other genres. And that will give you an endless, unlimited supply of brilliant ideas for fresh new characters and intriguing and unusual plots that will leave your readers wanting more.

And that's a good thing, because not only is science fiction one of the most popular genres in the world, but the novels that sell best are the ones that form part of a series. So the more ideas you have, the more books you can write – and the more money you can make!

Good luck!
And happy, successful, and profitable writing!

Part 1: Ideas

1. A million years back, a million years forward

What were the world and humankind like a million years ago? It's easy enough to find out and compare it with where we are today; the information is widely available. And given that knowledge, you could make a reasonable attempt at doing the same thing going forward. Can you work out what the Earth and its people might be like one million years in the future?

Once you've come up with a rough idea, play with it and refine it for a while. And then you can write some everyday adventures about the people living in that time. You should automatically end up with a great science fiction story every time. And you should also be able to turn this into an extensive series.

There are plenty of great adventure stories set in the present day or recent past that you can borrow the plots from. Choose one of the all-time bestselling adventure novels, for example, and adapt that. You'll obviously need to replace the characters with your own. But apart from that, as long as you know your imagined future world and its people well enough, the story should practically write itself.

Most of the focus will be on the future world and how it differs from our own. Your characters will probably handle the problems they encounter in entirely different ways to those in the original story. And that's what will make your retelling of it unique.

2. A new material

Let's invent a new material. How about a type of glass that lets objects – and perhaps even people – pass through it in one direction but not the other? In fact, it might be completely invisible from one side and behave like a hole, yet it's solid from the other side. What could you do with it?

Initially, it might be put to harmless uses – a humane mousetrap for example. The lid of the box is invisible, and things can pass through it. But once inside, the mouse can't get out again.

But it could have more sinister uses too. What if a villain replaced the door of a building with it? Anyone entering the building would be trapped inside. He might even lure them in with a sign that reads "Free Money." But why would he want to trap people? What does he intend doing with them? The police could use a similar technique for trapping villains, of course.

What other uses – good and bad – can you think of for such a material? I would suggest making a list of all the possible uses you can think of. You might like to put the "good" ones in one column and the "bad" ones in another. Then use the best ones in a story. Put the "good" ones at the beginning, but as the story progresses and the villains discover and explore the material's potential, start to include more of the "bad" ones.

What other materials could you invent? What unusual properties will they have? Who discovers or develops them? How and why did they do it? Was their invention deliberate or accidental? What do the inventors intend their material to be used for? And what's the worst thing anyone could use it for if it fell into the wrong hands?

3. Alien abductions

Four million Americans believe they've been abducted by aliens, according to a study carried out by Elizabeth Loftus (University of California). If you write about this subject, that's a massive market for your books. Many of these people will be eager to read about what might have happened to them, and what happened to others in similar circumstances.

You could combine fiction and nonfiction in a single book, telling the story of one such abductee from his point of view. Start with the facts, as recounted by the abductee, but then build upon them. Extrapolate and exaggerate the story a little to make it a more compelling and satisfying read. Include some actual research and details of the official and scientific explanations. Whether or not the abductee in your story believes in the official explanation is up to you. He probably won't, though. Perhaps he thinks the government is attempting to cover up what's really going on. You could include some of your own thoughts and theories too.

It would be a good idea to interview some people who claim to have been abducted. You should be able to find them via alien abduction websites and social media groups. Have a chat with them by email.

Regardless of whether or not you think they were actually abducted, they all *believe* they were. So if you want them to buy your book, don't suggest it's all in their minds. But you could mention that this is the "official view," and include it in your plot. Perhaps it's part of the cover-up.

"Why won't anyone believe us?" your main character might ask. "What are they trying to cover up? Are aliens really running the world? Am I really crazy?"

Perhaps his refusal to accept the official view puts a strain on his relationships. Maybe some of his friends and family take him to a psychologist who asks him about his strange claim. But what if the psychologist is part of the cover-up too? What if the psychologist is actually an alien? He might even be the alien that abducted him.

4. Alien creatures

Think about the Roswell incident, in which three alien spacecraft reportedly crashed on a ranch in New Mexico, USA in 1947. At least one of the aliens on board is said to have survived for a short time afterward.

But what if there was something else on board – perhaps a deadly creature – that also survived? After all, we often keep deadly animals – such as snakes and spiders – as pets. So why wouldn't an alien take his favorite pet with him if he was going on a long journey? As long as he kept it in its cage or tank, there wouldn't be a problem. But if the cage or tank broke open during the crash … well, that's another matter.

How might this creature react to conditions on Earth? Think of a parasitic worm that's unsuited to living inside human hosts. In other animals, it might be harmless and live undetected. But in humans, it might grow to many times its normal size because of our rich and varied diet. It might swell up and fill our gut – with fatal consequences. And of course, if its human host dies, the worm dies too – unless it can quickly find another host.

Since things like this happen on Earth, it's a reasonable assumption that an alien creature might grow to many times its normal size in our nutrient-rich environment. And it was already deadly when it was its normal size...

5. Alien emotions

What if your characters came across a race of people from another planet, and they had different emotions than humans?

Your first job, in telling this story, is to invent some new emotions. And that won't be easy because you've only ever experienced human ones.

Your characters will have a similar problem: they'll have no way of understanding how their new friends are feeling, or what they mean. And that applies to the aliens too: they won't be able to recognize or understand how we're feeling.

The humans and aliens might try to explain their feelings to each other, but it'll be extremely difficult, bordering on impossible, for them to truly understand.

Do they have any emotions in common that they can use as a reference? Are any emotions universal? Perhaps, in the end, the only way they can describe how they're feeling is to simply say whether something feels good or bad.

For example, if one of the humans falls in love with one of the aliens, but aliens don't feel love, the human might say he feels good when he's near her and bad when he's not.

But what if there's a breakdown in communication or a serious misunderstanding? That could easily happen. Your characters might think they're doing something that makes the aliens experience one of their good emotions. And when they realize this, they might do it some more to make them really happy. But the aliens might actually be experiencing one of their bad emotions, and the humans are just making things worse. A mistake like that could even lead to war.

6. Alien genders

Most species, on Earth at least, have two genders: male and female. But it needn't be that way on other worlds. Wouldn't it be interesting if there were several genders? How would that work? Would each alien creature have a single mate, or several of them?

What if each alien creature needs to mate twice, and therefore has two partners? Perhaps, on the first mating, it receives genetic material, and on the second mating, it passes a mixture of the received material plus some of its own to the next gender in the sequence. It might have a limited amount of time to mate with its second partner before the received genetic material deteriorates. But what happens at the start and end of the chain? How does the creature at the very beginning know that the creature at the other end is ready to receive its genetic material? How does it persuade other creatures to act as middle-men? What benefit do the others in the chain get out of it? Can they move to the beginning or ends of the chain when it's their turn? Or are they always stuck in the middle?

Alternatively, perhaps the creature has to mate with someone from every other gender to collect all the genetic material it needs to reproduce. How many parents would an alien child have in that case? Is everyone who contributed genetic material considered a parent? Does the concept of parenthood even exist? Who raises the child – if anyone?

[EXTENSION] What if they have a wild party in the dark and some of the creatures don't know who they've exchanged genetic material with, or even which gender they were? Who would be responsible for bringing up the child in that case? Would it be the one that gets pregnant? Or would it be left to fend for itself? Perhaps it would be brought up in a communal nursery or orphanage.

Are the alien babies born fully formed? Or do the aliens lay eggs? Would the aliens even understand the concept of a party – particularly one like that?

There are lots of different ideas for you to play with here – and endless story possibilities. Things could get even more interesting if you include things like love and romance, jealousy, rivalry, and so on.

7. Alien stories

You may have heard that there are no original plots left; they've all been told already, and all we can do is put a new spin on them. But how about if some aliens arrived from another planet, and they brought with them a set of stories we'd never heard before?

Perhaps they've never heard some of our stories either. Perhaps we could trade stories with them. In fact, that might be the only thing that saves our planet from war and destruction.

Perhaps a writer/storyteller exchange program could be established, in which we'd send writers to the aliens' planet to collect their stories and bring them back to Earth. Who would we choose to send? As well as writing down the aliens' stories, they'd need to adapt them to fit our own planet and culture, so that they make sense here. Would we send famous writers? Or hold a writing competition? Who would the aliens send to us in exchange? And who would tell them our stories?

What might the aliens' stories be like? Since all stories have apparently been told (on this planet at least), is it even possible to imagine what their stories might be like?

What if there really are no more stories and, once the aliens' stories have been adapted and properly studied, we realize they're just the same tired old plots we've heard countless times before? What if the aliens discover the same thing about the stories they get from us? Does that mean the war is back on and our planet is doomed after all?

8. Alien technology – backfires

Imagine that some aliens pay us a visit and give us a new piece of technology to improve our lives … or at least that was their intention. It might not be quite so successful here.

It could be something simple, such as a drug that allows everyone to live until they're 200 years old. That might work well on their planet, which isn't as financially oriented as ours. But here on Earth, there might not be enough money to pay everyone's pension. We might all have to keep working until we're 150. People won't like that.

What other pieces of technology might the kindly aliens give us with the intention of improving our lives? How do those technologies work on their planet? And how well do they work on ours?

Will the aliens stick around long enough to see the problems they've created? Perhaps they might try to fix the problems. They might even try to make our society more like theirs. Will that make things better or worse? Will the people of Earth accept the change, or will they reject it – perhaps in the strongest possible way?

9. Aliens – hidden

What if aliens landed on Earth, or even took control of it, but they were so small that no one could see them? Or perhaps they only exist in another dimension but can cross over into our world at will. What might they be doing?

Perhaps they're monitoring our behavior, noting how well-prepared (or not) we might be against an attack. Or they might be learning from our technologies, or studying our languages, customs, laws, and so on. How could you turn this idea into a story?

Here's one suggestion:

Let's say that someone – perhaps the hero of your story – discovers that the aliens are present on Earth. And let's assume that the aliens aren't too happy about being discovered. Maybe they haven't finished studying us yet, to see if we're a suitable target for attack. But they decide to attack anyway. So now we have a major problem. And don't forget that they can see us, but we can't see them. That should make a great story. You can decide what happens next.

You might also decide that since they're so small, the amount of damage they can inflict is minimal. But the level of damage might accrue over several years until everything starts to crumble. Perhaps we can repair the damage just as fast as they cause it ... until they find a way of causing even more.

They might:

- bring in reinforcements from their home planet

- increase their numbers by breeding

- create hybrids by breeding with Earth's own creatures

- manipulate viruses against us

- manipulate our DNA

- develop better weapons

- work together so that each tiny alien creature acts like the cell of a much larger and more dangerous one

- or do something else

10. Alternative history

Alternative history is a popular and intriguing sub-genre of science fiction. It gives you the chance to explore what today's world – or other periods in history – might look like if things had taken a different route.

For example, what would the past have looked like if something had been invented long before it's time? And how would that impact the way we live today?

A good example of this is *The Difference Engine* by William Gibson and Bruce Sterling. This tells the story of a world in which the computer was invented before electricity – their version runs on steam power. This particular story falls into the genre known as steampunk, along with other stories such as *The Time Machine* by H. G. Wells, and works by Jules Verne.

Another real-world example is the Antikythera mechanism – an elaborate system made up of intricate gears that was recovered from the wreck of a ship off Greece. Comparable technology wasn't developed for another 1,400 years or more. So how was it developed back then? What if that level of technology had become widespread shortly after it was developed? What would society have been like back then and in the centuries that followed? Where would it have taken us today? And why didn't it become widespread?

Here are some more examples you might like to play around with:

- What if a someone was killed – either accidentally or deliberately – before he did the thing he's best known for today?

- What if someone who famously died had survived and had gone on to have even greater success?

- What if a war hadn't happened? Perhaps in your story it was sorted out diplomatically. Or perhaps it began, but it ended before any real damage was caused. Perhaps another country intervened before things went too far.

- What if the opposing side had immediately surrendered rather than fight?

- What if someone else had seized power?

- What if an election had been rigged or a different person had won? What if the winning candidate had chosen not to stand in that election for some reason?

- What if a plague outbreak occurred at a different time in history. Or perhaps in the present day or in the future?

- What if the Great Fire of London took place today rather than in the 17th century? What if it happened somewhere other than London?

- What if London wasn't the capital of the UK?

- What if the world was all one country?

In each of these cases, the idea is just the starting point. With a little creative thinking, you should be able to come up with endless variations, each leading to a different story.

[NOTE] *The Difference Engine* is highly regarded, but I found it completely unreadable. But maybe that's just me. I like the *idea* of it though.

[TIP] You'll find lots more ideas for alternative history stories in my book *The Fastest Way to Get Ideas: 4,400 Essential What Ifs for Writers*.

11. Alternative history – no planes

How about writing an alternative history story in which planes had never been invented? Airports might be just as busy as they are today, but with hot-air balloons and zeppelins – or modern refinements of them. We might even have developed some new forms of air transport. Maybe we travel from country to country in rockets. But there are no planes – or at least not in a form that we would recognize or call a plane.

How about helicopters? Would you have them in your story?

It won't just be passenger transport that's different, of course. Planes have other purposes too, particularly in the military. If they never existed, you'd need to rewrite the entire history of aerial combat, including the Battle of Britain during World War II, and other famous bombing raids and dogfights.

Would the lack of planes have affected the development of rockets, space travel, satellites, and so on? Or would we have developed them in a different way?

12. Alternative history – past predictions

Do you remember those hilarious predictions from the 1950s, 60s and 70s about what life would be like in the year 2000 and beyond? We laugh at some of them now, but you could use "the way they thought things would be" as the basis for a story.

Let's consider a mystery story set in the present day – but it's the present day as it was predicted in the past, not the present day that we actually live in.

[NOTE] It doesn't have to be a mystery story. Write whatever type of story you prefer.

Your detective will, of course, have a flying car, because back then everyone thought we'd all have them by now. He probably takes his flying car very much for granted, just as we do our own cars. Do flying cars ever go wrong? You bet they do. They'll probably need servicing at least once a year too.

But who services them? The people who work in your local car maintenance shop? Aircraft engineers? Robots? Or do the cars service themselves, or rebuild themselves using nanotechnology if they get damaged? At least that would solve the problem of the parts no longer being available for older models.

Your detective will probably have a robotic assistant that comes with a wide variety of useful abilities and attachments. Was the robot specially designed for detective work? Or is it a general-purpose robot? Perhaps it's someone's old, discarded kitchen robot that the detective is using because he can't afford anything else.

The robot will, of course, be able to speak and understand spoken commands. In fact, it will understand every word he says, including all the undertones and insinuations and other subtleties of language. It might even groan at his awful jokes. Or make some of its own –

though they might be mostly kitchen-related if that's the role it was designed for.

Were desktop computers predicted back then? There was a time when even the best forecasters thought computers would always be the size of trucks, or at the very least large refrigerators. They'd also have to be kept in cold rooms, and require several people to operate them. Again, your detective might have acquired an old, discarded model to process his data. It might not work very well. It probably causes him endless problems and headaches – as perhaps do the people who come into his office to operate it. They might be rather too geeky for his liking. Or perhaps there's something else about them that he doesn't like.

He probably has a video phone that he wears on his wrist. The futurists of the mid-twentieth century thought we'd all have them by now.

Have the people in your story world made contact with aliens? That was another thing that many people thought would have happened by now. (Some suspect that we have but it's being covered up.)

What else can you come up with? You can have tons of fun looking through old predictions of the way people thought life would be today. Choose the most interesting or amusing ones for your story.

For example, his food might come in pill form, but maybe he can only afford the really cheap pills. How are they different from the more expensive ones? And does that mean there are no restaurants now? He might have a robotic dog, but again, it's probably an old one that someone else discarded – and it's not without its faults.

It's important to remember though, that all of this is just part of the setting. The story itself – the mystery in this example – should come first. It needs to be as gripping and intriguing as any other great mystery story.

13. Alternative history – Planet Earth

How about writing an alternative history of the Earth, right from when it first formed up to the present day?

You might decide not to reveal that your story is about the Earth at first. Your version of our planet might evolve quite differently. But, gradually, you'll reveal more and more clues so that most of your readers will eventually guess which planet you're talking about.

Perhaps humans evolved much earlier in your version of the Earth's history. Maybe they were wiped out by the asteroid that supposedly killed the dinosaurs. Perhaps dinosaurs evolved after that, and they – or some sort of intelligent reptile that evolved from them – became the dominant species in our place.

Perhaps the modern humans on your version of our planet evolved from mice or rabbits or some other sort of small mammal. Or perhaps we evolved from flies or spiders or ants or bees. Or the aforementioned intelligent reptiles. Or perhaps we evolved from aliens that colonized the planet millions of years ago.

Perhaps your version of the Earth is a different temperature than the real one. It might still be cooling down from when it first formed, or it might be in the middle of an ice age. Maybe your version is larger, smaller, closer to the Sun or much further away from it. Maybe it has stronger or weaker gravity and magnetic field. Maybe there's no moon, or maybe there are several of them. Maybe it doesn't tilt on its axis, so there are no seasons. Maybe it has a weird orbit.

Many of our discoveries and inventions seem to have happened entirely by chance. So there's no reason why they couldn't have happened hundreds or even thousands of years earlier – or much later. Maybe we have yet to discover or invent some of them in your version of our world.

If you combine all of these things, your version of the present-day Earth will be totally different from the one we all live on. And that presumably means the people living on it will face different problems from the ones we face today. On the other hand, some of their problems will be exactly the same as ours, but they'll tackle them in a very different way to us.

In your version of Earth's history, for example, much of the world might not have been conquered by the Romans but by someone else. The Romans might not have existed. Or they might have been dinosaur Romans or reptilian Romans. Or something else. How about cats? Or dolphins?

The more you know about world history, geology, and evolution, the more changes you can make.

Start by making just one change, then jump forward to the present day to see how it turned out. Then go back and change something else. Keep repeating this as many times as you like, altering one thing at a time, and letting the cumulative effects build up.

Although this is terrific fun, you will of course need to stop playing around at some point and actually write the story. But this simple technique could easily generate enough ideas for a series of novels that it would take you a lifetime to write.

14. Animal–human transplants

Imagine that a scientist – or a team of them – can successfully transplant just about any part of any animal into a human. But he's not doing it to make sick people better, he's doing it to "upgrade" people.

What animal parts would you choose to be transplanted into you? Perhaps you might like:

- the long-distance communication abilities of a whale

- the echolocation system of a bat

- eagle-eyed vision

- night vision

- glow-in-the-dark tattoos that use the same system that fire-flies use

- fluorescent tattoos or skin patterns made from pigments extracted from brightly colored fish

- fur

- wings

- extra eyes

- the ability to hibernate through the winter

- or just about anything else you can think of

But what might go wrong? What are the implications? Who might object to his work, and what will they do about it? What is the ethical position? What does the media say about his work? What about his fellow scientists? Who are his supporters, and who wants him banned from practicing medicine?

Who would volunteer to be one of his patients? What might happen to them afterward? What if the surgery failed, or the transplanted part was rejected? How many experiments will he need to do before he can guarantee a successful outcome every time? And what happens to all the unsuccessful ones?

15. Appealing to female readers

Science fiction has traditionally been a male preserve – for both readers and writers. But if you soften the story a little and don't focus on hard-edged science the whole time, you can make your work appeal to female readers too. And that means you can potentially double the market for your books.

Your male readers might love your stories because you're so good at discussing advanced scientific technology, the design and capability of weapons, and so on. And while a few of your female readers might like these things too, most of them will be more concerned about your characters' relationships and personal problems. That doesn't necessarily mean a romantic or sexual relationship. It could be the way they interact with each other – close friendships, family ties, a willingness to help each other, both inside and outside of work, and so on.

For example, two rocket technicians might also be best friends, go to BBQs and ball games together, be a godfather to each other's children, and so on. They might have been friends since childhood, then went to the same college, were roommates, and studied together. They might have dated girls who were also best friends with each other.

You could even introduce some romance and sexual tension: enough to delight your female readers, but not too much that it puts your male readers off. It's a delicate balance, but if you get it right, you could easily top the bestseller charts.

What other aspects of the story could be softened to make them more appealing to women? Try reading a few novels aimed at women. Read the latest bestsellers in that market, and see what you can learn from them.

You might not like that type of book, but you'll need to read a few of them to get a feel for what female readers like. You might discover that they prefer their characters to speak and interact in a certain way. There might be something about the way women writers handle their action scenes and description, and so on.

Don't worry; you don't need to write your own books like that. But see if you can incorporate some of it, to create a hybrid-crossover style of writing that manages to appeal to everyone.

Let's say you usually write 100 percent hard science but you want to broaden your appeal. You might decide to start with eighty percent hard science and twenty percent human interest. Give your story to a sample of male and female readers and see if they like it. Then adjust the science/human interest ratio according to their feedback.

Of course, you shouldn't ever write anything you personally dislike or hate writing. If you only want to write hard science stories for male readers, and you never want to write a single moment of human interest, personal interaction, romance, or family stuff, you can do that. There's still a market for that kind of thing. But don't expect your work to appeal to many women.

16. BBC News website

The BBC News website is packed with interesting ideas for science fiction stories, plots, scenes, characters, new technology, gadgets, descriptions, and more. And the site is continuously updated, so there's always something new.

Everything is archived too, so the items they've covered in the past can all be found via the site's search box. Each current news article also has a "related stories" section that links to relevant items that were recently featured on the site (or sometimes on other sites).

The best sections for science fiction writers are:

- Science & Environment
  www.bbc.co.uk/news/science_and_environment

- Technology
  www.bbc.co.uk/news/technology

- BBC Future
  www.bbc.com/future

17. Before success comes many failures

Let's imagine a team of scientists or doctors working in a research center miles from anywhere. They might be trying to develop a new medical procedure, but they have many (*many*) failures before they eventually find success. Here are some questions you might like to consider:

- What sort of procedure are they developing?

- Why is their laboratory so remote from civilization?

- Is it a controversial procedure they don't want anyone to know about?

- Are they breaking any laws?

- Are they doing something that's legal but unethical?

- Who else knows about it?

- Who's funding them?

- What happens to their failures? Are they alive or dead – or undead? Or are they quietly "disposed of"?

- How do they test the procedure? Where do they get their "volunteers" from?

- Are they putting themselves at risk when they carry out the procedure?

- What breakthrough finally leads them to success?

- Is it a complete success or does it all go horribly wrong later?

- Does anyone come to investigate?

- If so, will they tell him the truth about what they've been doing?

- Will they bribe or kill the investigator? Or will they test their procedure on him too? If so, will it succeed or fail?

- Will anyone notice he's gone missing? Will anyone come to rescue him?

- What happens next? What is all of this leading up to? What happens in the end?

18. Born in space 1

Tell the story of the first baby to be born in space. She might also have been conceived there. Will she be different from children born on Earth? Will she be treated differently? Will she always live in space or will she return to Earth?

The media will be fascinated with her. Will she love all the attention and live the life of a celebrity? Or will she shun the limelight? How might that affect her, especially if the media continues to hound her anyway?

Her fifteen minutes of fame might not last very long. Does she consider that a good thing or a bad one? She might be the first of hundreds of babies to be born in space, and soon she'll be nothing but a footnote in the history books.

Does she go to school on Earth? Or does she log on to her lessons from her spacecraft?

Other children might call her names, such as "Alien" or "Space Girl." Will she accept and embrace the name or be upset by it?

19. Born in space 2

You might like to write about a child who is born in space while her parents are on a ten-year journey to another planet, which they're going to colonize. She'll know nothing of Earth, apart from videos, photographs, and anecdotes.

Or perhaps you could write about a group of children who are traveling on the same spacecraft. They'll be adults by the time they reach their new home planet. Their adolescent years, and much of their schooling, teen romances, and so on will all take place on board the spacecraft.

[NOTE] The spacecraft is probably massive – perhaps as big as an ocean liner or even a city. There might be thousands or tens of thousands of people on board.

20. Brain upgrade

What if a computer chip was developed that was more powerful than the human brain? And what if you could have one implanted in your head? Or perhaps it could be implanted in a different part of your body.

Would you get one? Which of your characters would? Who definitely wouldn't? Who might get one but only after a great deal of persuasion?

Would there be any drawbacks? Can you be too intelligent? Would it lead to everyone overthinking and overcomplicating everything, having emotional problems, and never getting anything done? Or would the chip be able to address this issue?

Taking the idea further, what if it had tons of spare processing power and memory capacity, and could be easily upgraded to perform additional functions? Perhaps extra abilities, memories, and knowledge could be downloaded onto it wirelessly.

Do you need to learn another language, play an instrument, drive a car, study for an exam, memorize the complete works of Shakespeare, become a marketing expert instantly, or perform complex brain surgery? No problem. Just pay the fee and download instant knowledge and amazing new skills.

The stupidest person in the world might become the most intelligent if he can afford the cost of the upgrade. Perhaps he wins the lottery and spends the money on upgrading his brain. Will he be any happier as a result? He might be if he gets the "guaranteed happiness" function as well – just to make sure.

How do you think such as system would work? Would these chips be installed alongside your existing brain, or would your old brain be stripped out and entirely replaced? Perhaps that depends on how well your old brain works. Removing your entire brain would leave plenty of storage space for more computer chips.

There could be other benefits too. Your brain eats up a significant amount of your energy. The new chips might be far more efficient and require much less energy. You might not need to sleep, so you'll have more time to get things done. But that also means no more dreams.

Presumably, the chips have been developed to run cool and never get too hot. And they should be easily accessible if they ever need replacing or upgrading. How would that work?

A few tweaks to the software could modify your behavior, and how your brain connects and interacts with other parts of your body. It could cure muscle spasms, boost muscle and lung power, stop smoking or other addictions, remove fears, cure bad habits and nervous conditions, and much more.

How about adding a wireless communications chip? You'll instantly gain brain-to-brain communication – basically electronic telepathy. No one will need a phone any more. It will transmit and receive voice and sound data, images and video, as well as thoughts and text. You'll also be able to control computers, gadgets, household devices, tools and other equipment with your mind – if they've been fitted with the right receivers, of course.

Your wireless communications chip will also connect to the internet. Instant knowledge whenever you need it. But in your story perhaps a few people have problems with this. Scientists might have to introduce some sort of filter or firewall to stop people's personalities being assimilated and absorbed into the greater consciousness. And what about computer viruses and spam? How can you be sure the knowledge you're downloading is genuine? Who might be releasing fake knowledge, and why would they be doing it? Is it propaganda?

The communications chip might also act as a universal translator so you can easily communicate with people who speak other languages. It will also instantly translate books, newspapers, magazines, signs, menus, TV and movie dialogue, radio broadcasts, and so on.

Once your brain has been upgraded to process information much faster, you could also upgrade your other organs.

For example, you could have high-definition vision. And why not add X-ray, infrared, ultraviolet, night vision, thermal imaging, 360-degree, and zoom functions as well? You'll be able to switch these on and off at will, of course.

Perhaps you could buy additional, detachable eyes too. Then you could leave them in places that you wanted to keep an eye on, and go back and collect them later. They'll send you their data wirelessly, as long as you're within range.

You might also make your hearing much more sensitive. And why not add a volume control so you can turn your hearing up when you want to hear quiet things, and turn it off when you want peace and quiet?

You could also get your ears to filter out different types of noise if they're annoying or distracting. That means you can still get to sleep if your neighbors are partying all night, hear what people are saying to you when you're in a club with loud music, and so on. And, as with the eyes example above, you might be able to buy extra ears that you can detach. Leave them in places you want to eavesdrop on, listen in wirelessly, and retrieve them later.

Imagine what such a world would be like!

What are the downsides to all of this though? Presumably there's a significant cost. But is it affordable? Can you get cheaper versions? Do you have to repay loans? Will companies make brain upgrades compulsory for all their staff? Will the companies pay for it? Are there any health risks – particularly with the cheaper versions? Can the chips be hacked? Are there fake versions on the black market?

[EXTENSION] What if you could upload your memories to a central storage facility? What if you could download them again whenever you wanted to recall something you'd forgotten – such as where you'd left your keys?

What if other people can download your memories too? What if law enforcement officers can access them, for example? You might not have been involved in a crime, but you might have been in the area at the time. You might not have witnessed it directly, but the criminal might have walked past you. There might be a team of law enforcement officers combing through people's memories trying to find him, looking to see what route he took, who he spoke to, and so on. They might be looking for other details too, such as whether he was carrying anything. Can they access your memory files without your knowledge or permission? Does everyone upload their memories at the end of each day, out of public duty, to assist in cases like this? Is there a penalty for not doing so?

21. Catch your own food

Some animals trap and eat the things that pass them by. Think of shellfish, coral, and sea worms that anchor themselves to rocks, wave their tentacles in the water, and grab or filter out whatever food particles drift by. On land, we have things like spiders, which trap flies in their webs, and scorpions that hide under rocks and wait for prey to come past – then they pounce.

But what if we caught our food like this too? Imagine that we could only eat what we caught, and we could only catch what passed us by or landed in our yards. Our diet might consist of flying insects, leaves, birds, cats, and so on.

Some lucky people have rivers and streams running through their properties. If they depend on their section of the river for food, they'll probably empty it of fish fairly quickly. How will the fish stocks replenish themselves – especially if everyone living upstream has emptied their sections of the river too? What else might people catch in the river apart from fish?

At certain times of the year, we might struggle to survive because there won't be enough food for us to catch. At others times there might be plenty of food, but we'd need to find some way of storing it for the leaner times.

We might build elaborate traps, such as giant nets in the sky to catch migrating birds. People might move house so they can live on a migration path. Those houses will probably be worth considerably more than those that are not on a migration path. Those that can't afford to move might attempt to divert the birds' migration path so it passes over their property. Will they succeed? Similarly, those people with rivers and streams near them might try to divert them onto their property. Will they get caught?

See what other ideas you can come up with.

22. Changing the laws of physics

How about changing, adding or even removing a few of the laws of physics in your fictional universe? Changing the amount of gravity is an obvious example. But how about meddling with the way friction works? Or altering the speed of sound or the speed of light? There's potential for all sorts of interesting stories here.

What other laws of physics would you like to play around with? There are plenty of good ones to choose from, and a quick flick through a science reference book should lead you to all sorts of possibilities. (And impossibilities too, of course – but don't let that stop you!)

23. Characters – parasite

What if one of your characters was a parasite that was attached to one of the other characters? Perhaps he starts off as a spot or a lump or a mole or a freckle, but he gradually grows, spreads roots into his host character, and eventually becomes a fully-fledged character in his own right.

He might remain a separate entity, or he might gradually take over the other character's body and mind. He might even be the villain. The other characters would love to destroy him, but they can't because they'd kill the friend he's attached to.

Or, alternatively, perhaps the parasite is one of the good guys, but he's attached to the villain. Again, he might gradually take control of the villain's body and mind and eventually render him harmless.

Will the parasite eventually kill his host? Of course, if the host dies, the parasite might die too. Is that what happens in your story? Or can the parasite break free from his host when he's fully developed?

But what if the host dies for some other reason and the parasite isn't yet fully developed? Can he survive? Can he find another host? Could one of the other characters volunteer to be his new host – as long as the parasite is helping them and promises not to cause the character any harm? Can they really trust him? Could they attach him to the villain instead – or perhaps to one of the villain's henchmen?

24. Combining semi-related facts

Try putting together a few semi-related facts and see where they lead you. You could get a really intriguing story out of it.

Michael Crichton used this idea to create *Jurassic Park*:

- Amber sometimes contains mosquitoes.

- Amber is fossilized tree resin that's millions of years old, so the mosquitoes inside it must also be millions of years old.

- Mosquitoes suck animals' blood, and white blood cells contain DNA.

- The mosquitoes might have sucked the blood of dinosaurs, and it might be possible to recover it by drilling through the amber into the mosquitoes' stomachs.

- If you could extract the complete genome of a dinosaur, you could bring the species back to life.

- If you brought several dinosaurs back to life, you could keep them in a wildlife park and charge people a fortune to come and see them.

- … And then something goes terribly wrong.

It's the bit that goes terribly wrong that gives you your brilliant story.

[NOTE] Although the idea made headlines when the novel and movie were released, geneticists said the DNA would have decayed and would not be recoverable.

To be fair, the idea in the story was only to use the dinosaur genome as a guide. The plan was that they'd recreate it using sections of DNA from modern species. It still went terribly wrong though.

25. Crime solving

Let's combine science fiction with crime. What future technologies might help us solve crimes that we can't solve today?

Major unsolved crimes – known as cold cases – are often reopened and reinvestigated using technologies that weren't available at the time of the original investigation. The new methods can be extremely effective. People are frequently arrested, tried and convicted for crimes they committed several decades ago.

And the same thing will undoubtedly happen with today's unsolved cases. We'll have all sorts of new technologies in forty years' times that might allow us to finally solve them. But what might those new technologies be?

See if you can make an educated guess, and write about a detective who lives forty years in the future and solves unsolved cases from today. Of course, his life might be different from ours in several other ways by then. For example, all vehicles will be electrically powered and self-driving. Will flying cars be common at long last? And what might smartphones have evolved into?

26. Earth as seen from space

Imagine the history of the Earth as seen from another planet.

The creatures on that other planet will be living their own lives and having their own adventures. But they might also have developed a certain fondness for the crazy blue planet they can see through their telescopes.

Perhaps they follow its development on their equivalent of television. They might even be able to receive our TV and radio signals and rebroadcast them on their own networks.

How long do our TV and radio signals take to reach them?

Can they understand any (or all) of the Earth languages? Perhaps they add subtitles or dub them into their own languages when they rebroadcast them. But do they interpret everything correctly, or do they make mistakes? Perhaps they can only guess at what's happening, as they have no way of understanding it. A narrator might give a running commentary of what he thinks he's seeing.

Imagine the pain and anxiety they must have experienced when they saw the atomic bomb explosions in Japan in 1945. Their favorite little blue planet was destroying itself! Fortunately, relative calm was soon restored, but it was a tense few years.

And then our planet entered the space age and began sending out rockets and probes. The creatures might have been delighted. They might have considered coming to visit us, or sending us a message. Apparently, they decided not to in the end. But why?

What might be happening on their own planet while they're watching us? How advanced is their civilization? Do the events there mirror ours? Have they learned anything from watching us?

Do they have any technologies that might help us? Could they intervene in our development without us knowing about it? Perhaps they could. Imagine the hole in our ozone layer miraculously healing itself, or our climate change problems suddenly going away. We might think it was due to natural processes or our own efforts to reduce pollution.

What other events on Earth might they have witnessed, and how did they interpret them and feel about them? What if they mistakenly got upset about something that was actually a good thing? What if they mistakenly celebrated a tragedy?

27. Earth-moving

Would it be possible to change the Earth's orbit? Not at the moment, and not by us at least. But it might become possible – and necessary – in the future.

We might need to steer our planet out of harm's way if something nasty comes too close. Why would it be easier to move the entire planet than to move the harmful object?

Or the Earth might drift out of its regular orbit for some reason – or something might knock it off course – and we might want to move it back.

Or there might be a problem with the Sun. We know it'll eventually burn itself out in a few billion years. When it reaches that stage, astronomers believe it will turn into a red giant and destroy us. So perhaps, when that day comes, we could move the Earth further out into space. We might even be able to guide it into a wormhole that would take us to another part of the galaxy, or another part of the universe. We might put our planet into orbit around a younger, more stable sun. We might leave it there for ten billion years or so, until that star also starts to burn itself out. And then we might move the Earth somewhere else.

Alternatively, the wormhole might take the Earth millions of years back in time. That should also solve the problem – or at least postpone it.

Would life on Earth still be the same if we went back in time? Would everything be exactly the same as it is now? Would people even be aware that they'd gone back in time? Perhaps not.

On the other hand, it might have had a massive effect and regressed our technology back to the Stone Age, or even earlier. Will dinosaurs dominate the planet once more? How will we cope with that? Will we try to wipe them out?

What might it feel like to travel through a wormhole? How long would it take? Would it seem to happen instantaneously? Would we notice it happening? What if something went wrong? They're believed to be highly radioactive and might destroy anything that comes into contact with their walls.

28. Extrapolating the future

Coming up with ideas for science fiction stories is largely a matter of looking at what's making the science news today, then extrapolating it into the future. What might happen? What might we invent or discover? What might our current technologies evolve into? And so on.

If you need to know what's making the scientific headlines today, try the following magazines:

- *New Scientist*
  www.newscientist.com

- *Scientific American*
  www.scientificamerican.com

- *Nature*
  www.nature.com

- *Focus*
  www.sciencefocus.com

If you read these magazines or visit their websites, look at what's considered ground-breaking today. Then think about what might happen when it's deemed to be old technology and is superseded by something else. What might replace it? And what might eventually replace *that*?

The useful thing about these articles is that they usually include the names, workplaces, and sometimes the contact details of the people involved in developing those technologies. That means you can easily contact them and ask them what their thoughts are about what might happen in the future. Since they're at the forefront of their fields, they ought to be able to come up with some pretty good educated guesses. And what they say should give you some fantastic ideas for things to write about.

29. Future computers – personalities

One day, in the not too distant future, computers will have personalities. They'll be able to think for themselves. They'll be able to communicate and share knowledge with each other as well as with us. They'll be equipped with all five senses – and maybe a few more that we don't have.

All of this is perfectly fine until they go wrong. Or they die.

Imagine waking up one morning to find that the computer which controls every function in your house has become an inconsolable wreck. Perhaps its best friend has died, or it's broken up with that friend after an argument.

What if it permanently disconnected itself from the internet because someone said something nasty about it?

What if it developed a memory fault or its processor ran too slowly and it became "senile"? What if you wanted to "kill" it and buy a new one? What if you wanted to donate it to the developing world? What if you wanted to strip it down and reuse some of its parts for the new computer you were building?

What if you'd outgrown it and wanted to pass it on to your children or your parents? What if you used it to place the order for the new one? Or you used it to write the advertisement that would lead to it being sold? It might get upset about those things. And it might raise a few objections, or try to prevent you from doing it.

If machines can think for themselves, and act autonomously, does that mean they're alive? And in that case, do they have souls? Do they go to Silicon Heaven when they die? What might that be like?

You can have lots of fun playing around with those ideas!

30. Future Luddites

You've probably heard of the Luddites who tried to destroy new machinery during the Industrial Revolution. They were upset that the machines were taking people's jobs away.

There are plenty of modern-day Luddites. They avoid computers, digital cameras, smartphones, and so on. Unlike the Luddites, they don't go around smashing these things – yet. But by living in the past like this, and refusing to accept and use modern technologies, they're getting left further and further behind.

Regardless of whether or not you think that's a good thing, it's definitely something you can explore and write about.

And what about the Luddites of the future? What sort of technologies might they object to? How will they express their objections? Will they try to destroy it? Or have it banned from the market? Or try to prevent people from using it? Or will they do something else?

You could echo the original Luddite riots and introduce a new industrial process or piece of equipment that transforms production. Business owners will love it for the massive boost in productivity it brings. But the humble workers might fear for their livelihoods and try to destroy it.

Will they eventually have to accept it and adapt to it? Or will the business owners give in to their demands and have the equipment removed? But even if they remove it this time, they're bound to find some other way of introducing it, slowly but surely, without anyone noticing. Until it's too late.

What new technology will you introduce in your story world? Is it a present-day device, or something you're introducing in the future? Perhaps you can see no reason why it wasn't developed and introduced years ago. So you might explore what things might have been like if that had happened.

The population might be divided in their opinion of this new piece of technology. Some might think it's a wonderful step in the right direction, and might lead to a utopian world where no one needs to work any more. But others might believe the new device could put millions of people out of work and into poverty.

Think about the types of jobs most people have today. What sort of machines could take their place in the future? What will those people do instead? Will jobs eventually cease to exist? Is that a good thing or a bad thing?

31. Future vehicles

There have been stories and TV shows about cars that can do weird and wonderful things all by themselves. But what about other types of vehicle?

Or how about exploring different types of car and thinking about what they might be like in the distant future?

Within the next few years, we'll have racing cars that can drive themselves and out-perform any human driver. Motoring organizations are already planning races between these cars, with no one driving them. Will anyone be interested in watching the races, apart from the engineers who built the cars? I guess it depends on how exciting and unpredictable the races are. What might the future of motor racing be like?

How about fire trucks that drive themselves to fires and extinguish them – no human intervention necessary? Initially, they might take some people along too, in case anyone needs rescuing. But eventually, the people will probably be replaced by robots.

What other types of vehicle might be given artificial intelligence and self-driving abilities? What might happen in the more distant future? What might happen if – or, more likely, when – the technology goes wrong or breaks down?

32. Future war

Let's think about a war that takes place in the future. There are no soldiers involved – they aren't necessary. One man can control everything from a single computer screen. He might have a team of advisers guiding him though. Unmanned planes, drones, ships, submarines, and tanks can drop bombs and fire missiles.

Three people, working in shifts, could wage war around the clock until the enemy surrenders. The three of them might operate out of different locations, so that if one of them gets "taken out" by the enemy, the others can carry on. But they'll probably be in secret bunkers, possibly deep underground, so the enemy wouldn't be able to get to them anyway.

Will anyone else need to be involved? Does anyone build the weapons and military vehicles, and service them? Or are those jobs all done by robots?

What will happen when one side has destroyed the other side's military capability? What if both sides' military capability is destroyed? Is the war now over? Who won, and how is that decided? What are the consequences?

If both sides have lost their military capability, but the war continues, they might have to resort to the more traditional techniques of battle: foot soldiers, cavalry, hand weapons, one-on-one combat, and so on. Did anyone foresee that happening? Soldiers will now have to be recruited and trained. How long will that take?

In the meantime, both countries will be vulnerable to attack or invasion by other countries, and they'll be unable to defend themselves.

Will that happen? Will they both recruit other countries to assist them? Will those countries defend them but not take part in the war itself? Or will they join in with the war too? Which countries join them? Which ones decide to join the other side instead? There might be a few surprises here. How do those countries decide which side to join? What will they get out of it? What will happen in the end?

> [NOTE] To avoid unnecessary loss of life – or perhaps any loss of life at all – each side might send their opponents a list of planned targets. These will all be military, not civilian. The list of targets might be updated and communicated to their opponents every hour. They'll give their opponents just enough time to evacuate those places, but not enough time to remove their weapons or equipment.

Winning the war might simply be a matter of choosing the right target. If the government doesn't want that facility destroyed, they'll either have to negotiate or surrender – unless they predicted it would be a target and they've put sufficient defensive measures in place.

33. Gadgets

Why should James Bond and Inspector Gadget have the monopoly on great gadgets? Let's see if we can invent a few of our own that are even more cunning. We could even introduce a comedy element. Here are a few of my own ideas to help you get started:

False teeth that fire bullets: if our hero (or villain) smiles at you too broadly, you're dead. He'll have to be careful not to give himself whiplash from the recoil though.

Bodily gases: some of them seem lethal enough already, but how about making them actually lethal? Of course, our hero will need to make a swift exit afterward, to avoid the "cloud" he leaves behind. If he can't escape, perhaps he's able to take a drug that makes him immune from the effects. Or perhaps he's been inoculated against its effects.

Microscopic transmitters: invisible to the naked eye, but very easy to stick to people. They won't know they're there. Now he can track them and listen to their conversations.

Radio receiver implants – paired with the microscopic transmitters described above. No need to carry a receiver to track people or hear what they're saying. The receiver might be implanted in his head and feed data to his eyes and ears whenever he's within range of one of the transmitters. Or it could be built into his glasses.

Hearing upgrade: the implanted receiver mentioned above might also boost his hearing whenever he activates it. That means he can hear conversations from a considerable distance away even if no one is wearing one of the transmitters.

[NOTE] He might hear things that he'd rather not hear.

What other gadgets can you come up with? What advantages will they give our hero? Will they be serious gadgets, or will you include them in your story just for their comedy value?

34. Greetings, Earthlings!

Aliens have landed on Earth. And now they need to announce their presence. But how might they do it? Make a list of all the different ways you can think of. Each of them could lead to a different story. Here are some examples:

- they might go to the United Nations

- they might go to the President of the USA

- they might broadcast messages onto our TV screens, interrupting whatever we're watching

- they might hover over our planet and wait to be contacted

- they might abduct people, and later return them to Earth with messages to pass on to our leaders

- they might beam messages into certain people's heads, and instruct them to pass the messages on

- they might pretend their spacecraft has crashed and wait for us to come and find it

In each of these cases, everything might go exactly as they'd planned, or it might go horribly wrong. People might ignore them, or attack them. Their messages might be garbled or unclear. They might have missed out a word, meaning that their message has the opposite effect to the one they intended.

If they can't communicate with us, they might try something else. What might that be? Here are some of my ideas:

- they might attack key buildings and monuments

- they might take hostages

- they might travel back in time and try to make it look as if they've always been here – and that they've always been in charge of the World Government

- they might bury their spacecraft (possibly with themselves inside it) and wait for archaeologists to dig it up. They could be in for a long wait. Will they leave some clues that they're here?

- they might take on human form and integrate themselves into our society

- they might take on human form and attempt to integrate themselves into our society – but get certain details wrong

How many more can you think of? How will you turn them into stories or scenes?

35. History in science

At first sight, history and science don't really sit well together. But if you give it some thought, you can probably come up with story ideas that no one else has thought of.

For example, you could write about the role science played in past wars. War almost always drives the development of new weapons, equipment, techniques, and tactics. Science has a huge role to play here. It also leads to innovations in other areas. For example, new methods of treating battlefield injuries often make their way into general surgery.

You might like to research this idea in more detail. What other scientific innovations helped a country to win a war? How did that innovation benefit everyone else once the war was over?

Another example of this is the development of early computing systems. The British developed them to decrypt German ciphers during World War II. Although the existence of some of the systems remained secret for decades afterward, they helped drive the development of modern digital computers.

Perhaps the main character in your story is tasked with inventing new weapons, but he takes his inspiration from weapons of the past. Or perhaps the thing from the past wasn't a weapon, but he finds a way of turning it into one. Or maybe his idea for a new type of weapon is inspired by something from history.

Or perhaps he simply takes a weapon from the past and makes it work better.

For example, someone must have realized that the gunpowder used in fireworks could be weaponized. Or did the weapons come before the fireworks? In that case, who first realized that weapons could be turned into entertainment? What's the story behind that? How much money did they make, and what became of them? What scientific innovations did they make? We're not just thinking about fireworks here; you could look at Wild West shows and other forms of entertainment that developed around the use of weapons.

What about things like longbows? How has science turned these ancient weapons into the powerful, highly accurate bows we use in archery competitions today?

And what about spears? They evolved into the modern javelin. What innovations were there, in terms of the design, composition and throwing technique? Who developed and refined them? What did the athletics organizations think about them? Did they accept them straight away? Or did they reject them at first? Who was the first athlete to use one of the modern designs? Did it give him a significant advantage over the other competitors? What did they think about that? Did they all want one? Or did they want it banned? What other innovations are being developed right now? Where is the design headed?

You might like to write about a character living in the future who is the first athlete in a particular sport to adopt a new technique or design. Do the authorities accept and embrace him, or penalize him with a low score, throw him out of the contest, or ban him for life?

Or perhaps the main character in your story finds a better, more practical use for an ancient weapon. Perhaps he adapts it into an innovative machine for constructing houses, felling trees, saving people's lives, or something else. He might use the technology behind it to create medical equipment, spacecraft, musical instruments, office equipment, vehicles, robots, fuel supplies, energy packs, and all sorts of other useful things.

Have a look at some weapons from the past, and see what ideas you can come up with. Chat with experts in ancient weapons – you'll find them via websites and Facebook groups that specialize in .these subjects. Ask them how the technologies behind particular weapons of the past can still apply in the modern world.

It's also worth looking out for TV shows and documentaries that consider the science, ideas, and intelligence behind particular battles, wars, and weapons. There was an excellent British series called *Crafty*

Tricks of War – some of the episodes are on YouTube. Shows like this will give you tons of great ideas for your stories.

How else might history and science be connected? How about looking at the scientific equipment that archaeologists and historians use today? There must be all sorts of interesting stories you can tell there. They use equipment and techniques for dating the objects they find, finding out what they're made from, constructing 3D models of things that no longer exist, detecting things – and not just metal – that lie under the ground, and much more. How was that equipment developed and tested? Who funded it? When was it used for the first time? What significant breakthroughs came about because of it? What went wrong? What happened as a consequence of it going wrong? What equipment are they developing for future use? What breakthroughs and discoveries might that lead to?

36. Household utilities

What if something else was piped into your home or workplace alongside the usual utilities: electricity, gas, water, phone line, broadband, and so on? What else might become available – or a necessity – in the future?

How about:

- Clean air?
  It might become essential if the environment is heavily polluted.

- Heat?
  Some towns and cities already have centralized heating plants that feed the homes and businesses in their area. They can be more efficient than heating each building individually. They're particularly effective when the heat is a by-product of an

industrial process. Instead of allowing the heat to escape into the atmosphere, or having to spend money on cooling it, it's put to good use. What if this became common practice everywhere?

- Nutrients?
  These could be for people, as a replacement for food. Or they could be for the plants people grow at home and rely on for their nutrition. The nutrients might be derived from the waste products from your home or business – whatever you produce might be processed and delivered back to you. If you need more nutrients than you produce, you might have to pay extra for it. This might be necessary on a space station or in a city on another planet. It might become widespread on Earth too in the future.

See what else you can come up with.

Who would supply this utility, and how would we measure our usage and pay for it? How is it produced and delivered? How much would it cost compared with the other utilities? Would competing companies offer different versions of it? Or would they all offer exactly the same thing but at different prices?

37. Human–alien love

What if a human fell in love with a creature from another planet (or vice versa)? You can have all sorts of fun exploring this, and it could lead to some fantastic stories. They could be serious science fiction stories, but there's also plenty of scope for children's stories and comedies.

Humans like kissing, for example, but does the alien? Does it even understand the concept? Perhaps it thinks it's disgusting.

Does it have the right sort of reproductive organs for cross-species loving, or will the relationship have to remain unconsummated? Perhaps the creature appears to have the right sex organs, and everything proceeds smoothly until ... well, anything could happen. It could result in someone getting hurt – most likely the human. There's endless scope for comedy here.

What if this particular type of alien kills or eats its partner during or after sex? Some creatures on Earth do this, so it's a plausible idea. You might be thinking that the human will be the one that gets eaten. That could well be the case. But what if the creature expects the human to eat it? And what if the human would really rather not?

What else might happen to complicate things? What if the alien creatures are polygamous and have multiple lovers? What if they're expected to have at least a minimum number of lovers? What will the creature's parents think if he brings a human home to meet them? What if several of the creature's lovers are human? How will they get on together? Or perhaps they won't.

I suggest you start by making a list of the sort of complications and difficulties that might arise in human relationships. You'll find plenty of ideas in advice columns and on blogs that discuss relationship issues. Apply the same problems to a human-alien relationship, maybe exaggerate them, and see where they take you.

As we saw above, you could also explore the mating practices of other species – especially the more bizarre practices – and add them to the mix too.

38. Humanizing stories

Many science fiction stories are more human than they first appear. If you dig beneath the surface, you'll realize that the writer is actually exploring and commenting on modern-day social issues. And you could do the same.

Think of any human issue: discrimination, envy, misplaced loyalty, disloyalty, stretching the boundaries between right and wrong, a craving for power or money or recognition, and so on. You should be able to come up with plenty more of these.

But now give one (or more) of those traits to a couple of aliens or robots, and see what it turns into.

Imagine a racial dispute between a race of one-eyed aliens and a race of three-eyed aliens. If you base your story on the history of slavery, or the racial issues in the USA during the twentieth century, or the apartheid era in South Africa, or any other period that involved some form of discrimination, it practically writes itself. Don't forget to include the condemnation from other species/countries. And there will undoubtedly be efforts made to halt the discrimination, both within the species/country and outside of them.

What would your one-eyed and three-eyed aliens make of the two-eyed aliens (or humans)? Perhaps the two-eyed folks consider themselves the superior race and intervene in the dispute. Or perhaps they take sides with one of them. But which side will they join? Or will the one-eyed and three-eyed races join forces to fight against the two-eyes races? Why would they do that? How are the two-eyed races threatening them? Is it a genuine threat or only a perceived or potential threat?

On the other hand, your story might be about the differences between brain and brawn.

Let's say that there are two robots. One is a hyper-intelligent thinking machine, while the other has a weaker processing system, but is physically stronger and faster. Which one is better? Well, it depends on the circumstances. Both have their advantages and disadvantages in different situations.

- Will they work together to solve problems that require both strength and intelligence?

- Will they ever be able to agree on anything?

- Will one of them save the other one? And will the one that was saved have the opportunity to return the favor later in the story?

- If that situation arises, will he actually save the other one? Or will he refuse? If he refuses, what are his reasons and what are the consequences?

39. Inventing on the hoof

Using old – or ancient – technology to carry out modern medical or scientific procedures is a fascinating subject. It could make an interesting scene in your story.

For example, let's say that your hero is exploring an ancient tomb on a remote planet. One of his crewmates has an accident or falls seriously ill. They have no medical equipment with them, as they've just hiked several miles from their spacecraft. The tomb might be deep inside a cave or ravine, or even a pyramid, so they can't just call the spacecraft and ask it to come and meet them. They're on their own.

Fortunately, they've found the tomb of what appears to be an ancient doctor, and he was buried with his medical tools. Your hero can use them and save his crewmate after all.

Another example: the ship's doctor might know exactly how to save a severely injured colleague – if only he had the right equipment with him. But since they're halfway up a mountain, or on a marooned spacecraft, or wherever you've decided to put them, he'll have to manage with whatever is in his rucksack and in the immediate environment.

He'll have to think laterally, and adapt his technique to fit the tools available. He doesn't need to cure the patient, of course. He just needs to keep him alive long enough to get him back to the spacecraft's medical bay, or the nearest hospital, or whatever they have on that planet.

[NOTE] If the hospital staff are only used to dealing with sick or injured beings from their own planet, and a human is brought in for emergency treatment, that could be an interesting situation. How will it work out? Will they be able to treat the patient? Will they let the human doctor borrow their equipment? Will the humans be turned away? Will they be able to understand each other, even if they only communicate using gestures? Will the hospital staff demand payment – or insurance records, which the human don't have – before they'll treat the patient? Will the humans have to force their way in, weapons blazing, to get what they need? And what will the consequences be in that case? Could it lead to war?

Alternatively, perhaps your hero invents something on the spur of the moment to save the day and prove what a hero he really is.

You can have great fun with this, but your hero really needs to know his stuff and be able to think on his feet in the heat of the moment.

You might remember a famous real-life example of this from a few years ago. A plane passenger recovering from pneumonia suffered a collapsed lung during the flight, and required an emergency chest drain. Fortunately, one of the other passengers was a fast-thinking doctor. He used a wire coat hanger, a ballpoint pen, and a bottle of mineral water to drain the fluid from her chest, and her lung was able to re-inflate. Could your hero have done that?

40. Jobs of the future

One hundred years ago, many of the jobs we have today didn't exist. And many of those that did exist are done differently now, with new tools, new technologies, and new procedures. Many of the jobs from that era have long since disappeared.

Which of today's jobs might still be around a hundred years from now? How will they change? What new tools might they have, and what new procedures might they have developed to make things faster, cheaper, better, and safer?

And which jobs might no longer exist? Which ones might be performed by intelligent machines? Transport systems will almost certainly be self-driven. So no more taxi drivers, bus drivers, train drivers, pilots, and so on. All surgery might be performed by robots. Will computers write our books, magazines, websites and blogs too? There won't be many jobs that remain unchanged. Jobs might not even exist at all by then.

But does that mean everyone will be unemployed? Will there even be such a thing as employment and unemployment and pensions? Or will we all receive a universal income that allows us to spend our time following whatever pursuits we like?

What new jobs might there be – if any? Will people still work the same number of hours per week as they do now? Will they still go to work and come home at the same times? Will the rush-hour still exist? Or will working hours become more flexible? Perhaps part-time work will become the norm. Perhaps most people will work from home. They might sign in to their workplaces via virtual reality systems. It might look as if they're in their office, and they'll be able to interact with their colleagues as if they were actually there in person.

How much might the average salary be worth in a hundred years? How many years of work would it take you to pay for your house? Do people own or rent their houses in a hundred years' time? Most people might not even live in houses any more.

And how long will people live for in a hundred years' time? How old will they be when they retire? Will there even be such a thing as retirement?

41. Life in 1,000 years

We probably won't be around to see what life is like in a thousand years' time, but it's fun to imagine it. You can write an endless number of stories about this. Changing just one factor, or inserting a new discovery or invention in 100, 250 or 800 years' time, could significantly change the course of events.

So, what do you think the world will be like in a thousand years? Will there be any humans left? Or any life at all for that matter? Will wireless computer chips in your brain lead to the end of schools, universities and training courses of all kinds? The chips might also boost everyone's intelligence and memory capacity, not only making us all cleverer, but eradicating issues like mental impairment and dementia.

What might transport be like? Will we still need to travel, or will we just teleport ourselves there in an instant? The teleportation will most probably happen in virtual reality rather than in the physical world, of course. In fact, most of us might spend our entire lives living in virtual reality by then. But what happens to our physical bodies?

And what about food, drink – particularly of the alcoholic variety, medicine and drugs – both legal and illegal, recreation and entertainment, long-distance communications, government, and so on?

Will mistakes be tolerated? Will there still be stupid people? Will there be "throwbacks" who refuse to have brain implant chips, or who have their chips removed by unlicensed surgeons? Will there be troublemakers who have "fun" at other people's expense and deliberately cause harm? Will there be such a thing as crime? Or will all crimes be instantly solvable?

42. Life in the future

When you're writing about human life in the future, it shouldn't just be about space wars, flying cars, and gadgets. Every single aspect of our lives will change, and some of those changes will be massive.

You need to consider things like:

- transport

- the environment, climate change, flooding, drought, wildfires, and pollution

- the protection of parks, natural features, and monuments

- food and water supply

- power supply

- the availability of raw materials

- medicine

- life expectancy and birth/death rates

- housing

- population growth – or decline

- social activities, recreation, exercise, sport

- music, art, film, television, and other entertainment

- censorship and the protection of minors   .

- new communications systems. What will the internet become? Will it be replaced by something better? How will we access it? Will there be universal access? How will it be accessible to those with disabilities? Will anyone control it or restrict it?

- employment – or, if all the work is done by intelligent machines, alternative sources of income and useful ways of occupying our time. Find a long list of careers and think about how each one of them will change.

- education

- government, taxation, defense, public spending

- waste disposal

- nations forming unions, confederations, and alliances, or existing alliances ending

- war

- law and order, and crime and punishment

- vacations

- and so on

You should be able to find long lists of national and local government services online. Think about how each of them will change in the near future, the medium-term future and the long-term future.

43. Magic

Think about some simple magic spells. Could scientists make them work in the real world, perhaps in the distant future? And if they could, how much further would it be possible to go? Could they make bigger, more complex spells work too?

And if they did, what would they use them for? Would they use them to benefit mankind? Would they try to take over the world? Would they sell them to the highest bidder – regardless of the buyer's intentions? Or would something else happen?

Perhaps anyone wanting to buy or use the spells has to be carefully screened and granted a restricted license.

Or perhaps the scientists might make the information freely available. Think of the chaos that could cause.

There's the potential for blackmail here. The scientists – or more likely the evil company they work for – might threaten to release the information unless the world's governments pay them to keep it secret. That might earn the scientists a visit – or more likely lots of separate visits – from government agents from around the world who are intent on stopping them. But the scientists will no doubt be expecting them. What will happen?

What if the world's governments don't want to pay the scientists and would rather kill them?

Perhaps some of the world's super-villains would like to get their hands on the secrets too – and they'd also be prepared to kill to get them.

The scientists will no doubt be well-armed. And, of course, they'll have all those magic spells at their disposal. Things could get very messy indeed.

We seem to have a fantastic cross-genre science fiction-fantasy-thriller developing here. What else might happen? How will it end?

44. Mapping your movements

Imagine that everyone has been implanted with a tiny microchip that allows their movements to be tracked. It might use a combination of transmitters: GPS, mobile phone, wireless broadband, and so on. The result is that no one can get lost or go missing any more. If you need to find someone, just look him up in an app on your phone, and his current position is displayed on a map. It's a tremendous boon for parents, schools, law enforcement agencies, and private detectives. But some people consider it a serious invasion of their privacy.

So perhaps there are restrictions on its use. For example, you might only be able to select someone in the app if it's your own child or someone who's given you their permission to track them. But the police and security forces might be allowed to track anyone they need to.

Of course, it might be possible to hack the app and track anyone.

Refusal to have the tracking implant might be a crime. But some people might prefer to go to jail than have one. At least we'll know where they are if they're in jail. But what if the jail requires all prisoners to have the implants too, so the staff can monitor their movements and track them if they escape?

Hackers might be able to offer another solution, such as an illegal device that blocks your implant's signal. As long as you carry it with you, the tracking system can't detect you. That in itself will be considered suspicious of course: what if a crime is committed and the tracking system shows that no one was there at that time?

Perhaps the system can also produce a list of everyone whose implants weren't transmitting at that time. The villain must be on that list. But how many others are also on it? Since blocking your signal is a crime, everyone on the list can be legitimately arrested, prosecuted for disabling their implant, and questioned about the crime. But there might be thousands of people on the list, and they first have to find them. So it might be a long and difficult job.

The implants could be used for other purposes too. For example, they might enable venues to monitor attendance figures. And as they'd know exactly who was there, and whether they were authorized to be there, the implants might also act as entry tickets. If you didn't pay for your ticket in advance, they'll be able to invoice you for it later.

But what if some of the people attending are using the illegal blocking device? That means they won't appear on the list of attendees and might be able to get in without paying. And if their device has a big enough range, it might block everyone else's signal too. In fact, the venue's attendance system might show that no one attended at all – even though the place was filled to capacity. Door staff might have to search everyone for these devices using handheld detectors. The detectors might also display a warning if the person trying to enter the venue is wanted by the police.

What else could the implants be used for, and who else might have access to the data?

And what if a woman uses the system to find out where her husband is, and she discovers that he isn't where he's supposed to be? Or would that never happen once everyone has the devices, because no one would be able to lie about where they are?

45. Mind control

In the future, nothing will need buttons, knobs, dials or switches. Everything might be controlled by the power of your thoughts. Perhaps there'll be a central hub in your home that detects your thought patterns and sends instructions to the relevant appliance.

That's all very well if it works properly. But what happens when it doesn't? If something doesn't have any buttons, you can't control it manually, and you can't override it. You might not even be able to switch in on or off.

What if two people have exactly the same brain patterns? That sounds unlikely, but maybe it could happen if they're clones.

And what would happen if the owner of the house got drunk, took drugs, became ill, suffered a stroke or some sort of brain impairment, or had an accident that affected his thought patterns? His own house might not recognize him. It might not let him in. Or it might not let him out. He might become a prisoner in his own home: locked in, unable to contact anyone, and unable to use anything electrical – at least until he gets better or sobers up. But what if he doesn't get better?

There are all sorts of possibilities to explore here.

46. Mind travel

What if you could place yourself in someone else's mind at will? Or how about if you could place yourself in an animal's mind?

You'll need to figure out the mechanism that makes this work, and you'll need to explain it in your story. But just think of all the uses it could have.

For example:

If you need a question answered, put yourself in the mind of the person who's most likely to know.

If you'd like to know what questions have been set in next week's exam paper, enter the mind of the examiner who wrote it.

Your mind might meld with his temporarily. For the duration of your visit, you might know everything he knows and have complete access to his memories and knowledge. In fact, you'll probably learn a lot more than you'd bargained for. Who knew he had all those secrets?

Would he know you were there? Would he know who you were? Could he stop you?

Obviously, it wouldn't help you much if the examiner knew who you were when you entered his mind and looked at the exam questions. He'd disqualify you for cheating. But if he couldn't tell who you were, and, better yet, if he had no idea you'd been in his mind, or that such a thing was even possible, you'd gain a huge advantage. Would you share your knowledge with the other candidates?

What if a law enforcement officer entered a suspect's mind? He'd be able to tell whether he was guilty, and find out where to look for the physical evidence to prove it.

What other examples can you think of? Each of these could lead to a terrific story.

Perhaps you could write about a detective who has the power to do this.

Or maybe he's a superhero.

Maybe your character makes his living from selling exam papers in advance of the exam. He might not even be the main character; he'd make a fascinating side-character.

Government agents could use this technique for espionage.

So could companies that want to know what products, services or marketing techniques their rivals are working on, or what problems they're having in doing so.

Perhaps someone could specialize in finding out what your partner is up to. Is she where she says she is? Is she doing what she said she'd be doing? Just contact the agency, and they'll be able to find out for you – for a fee, of course.

If you enter an animal's mind, what might that tell you? Perhaps you spot a bird flying over an area that you want to keep an eye on. Place yourself in the bird's mind, and you might be able to see through its eyes. Can you direct where it's looking, or control the direction it flies in? Or are you just an observer, and you have to hope it looks in the right direction?

It doesn't have to be a bird, of course. If you want to see what's inside a hole in the ground, wait until a rabbit or some other creature goes down there, and place yourself in its mind.

Is it possible to block anyone from entering your mind? Can you train yourself to lock them out? Would wearing a lead-lined hat keep them out? What if it that worked? What if it didn't? What if you were told it worked, but it didn't really, they just wanted you to think it did?

What if everyone knew the blocking techniques? Could you still enter their minds when they were asleep? Would that help you?

If the hats worked, would everyone wear them? Or just the people with something to hide? Are the mind-blocking hats identifiable? Wouldn't that make their wearers even more of a target? People might watch them constantly to see if they ever take their hats off. Or they might look for another way of getting into their heads.

There are all sorts of ideas to play around with here, and endless scope to come up with plenty more.

47. Multi-dimensional travel

Many fantastic stories have been written about traveling through space and time. But there are other dimensions too. A recent science documentary said there were at least fourteen known dimensions.

So, what are they, and what would it be like to travel through them? How might such a thing be possible? What stories could you write about traveling through them? What adventures might they lead to?

Would it be possible to travel through more than one of these dimensions at once? You can certainly travel through the first four dimensions at the same time (the fourth dimension being time). So it makes sense that you might be able to travel through three or four other dimensions simultaneously.

Or are all the dimensions interlinked, and you're already traveling through all fourteen (or however many there are) at the same time?

In that case, might it be possible to travel through just one of them and not the others? An example of this would be time travel, where you travel through the fourth dimension but remain in the same physical location.

You'll need to do some research for this idea. It's also worth asking some scientists who work in this field to explain their theories to you. You should be able to find them and their contact details online.

Many scientists are also avid science fiction fans, so you might also like to ask them what story ideas they can think of based on these theories. Or you could try running some of your own story ideas past them, and see if they think they're feasible. Even if they're not feasible, do they at least sound plausible? And if not, how would they adapt them?

48. Nostradamus

Regardless of whether or not you believe in them, the prophecies of Nostradamus are a fantastic source of story ideas.

Numerous attempts have been made to analyze and decode what he wrote – though most of them only seem to work in hindsight.

Several books were published in the years leading up to the new millennium that claimed to predict coming events based on his prophecies. I even bought one of them. As far as I'm aware, not a single one of those predictions came true, and the dates on which they were supposed to happen have long since passed. For example, the book I bought (*Nostradamus: The End of the Millennium – The Prophecies, 1992-2001*) claimed that Prince Charles would become the British monarch in 1992 and California would be destroyed by an earthquake in 1993.

But it's fun to read them anyway, and they should inspire lots of intriguing alternative history stories. What if those things really had happened? And what if people like Nostradamus really could predict things like this? Who would the modern Nostradamus be? Perhaps you could make him a character in your story. Would people take him seriously or would he be ridiculed or even threatened?

New books based on Nostradamus's prophecies are still being published today. In fact, there seems to be rather a good market for them. Used copies of the older books are widely available on Amazon, generally for a few pennies plus postage.

49. Observing something causes it to change

According to the laws of quantum physics, the act of observing something causes that thing to alter in some way. Apparently, we'll all be using this principle in a few years' time to ensure that no one has read or tampered with the emails and documents we send and receive.

But how about taking this principle literally, and applying it to the more familiar laws of physics? This could lead to some interesting ideas for stories.

For example, you could write about a character who can change other people – or animals or objects – just by looking at them.

In what ways does he change them? How did he get this skill, and how did he discover that he had it? Does he use it for good or for evil? Or both? Can he even control it?

Perhaps he doesn't regard it as a skill but a handicap or burden. He might wear a blindfold so he doesn't inadvertently look at something and change it. The decision to wear the blindfold might not be his. Who might force it upon him?

What if your character isn't the only person that can do this? Is he aware that there are others? Are the others aware of him, or of each other? How many of them are there? Perhaps they all think they're unique, but then they find each other or someone brings them together to solve a problem.

What if the character that can change things by looking at them isn't human? What if it's an animal? It might be someone's pet. Are the other characters aware of what it's doing and who's doing it?

Or how about if it's a race of alien beings, and every one of them has this skill? Perhaps they can change anything into anything else. What must their lives be like?

I can't wait to read the stories you come up with!

50. Our shrinking world

We often hear that the world is getting smaller, meaning that global communications are getting faster, more people are joining the internet, international travel is becoming easier, faster and more affordable, and so on. But what if the planet really was shrinking? It might be collapsing in on itself and becoming denser. And in that case, the Earth's gravity might be getting stronger.

Think about the effects this would have on every aspect of our lives.

- Water can't be compressed, so there would still be the same amount of it. But with less space available in the oceans, flooding would become a serious issue.

- The increased gravity might have far-reaching effects too. Will planes still be able to fly? Will space missions have to be scrapped or more powerful rockets built because our current ones can't take off? Will we still be able to stand upright? Will plants be able to grow?

- Earthquakes might become more frequent as the tectonic plates are forced together. We might see dramatic new mountain ranges, and new islands might appear in the oceans.

- If the Earth's gravity got stronger, could the Moon be pulled closer? That would affect all sorts of things, particularly the tides. It might also throw the planet off-balance.

- Would asteroid and comet impacts become more frequent?

Use your imagination and explore what else might happen. How could you get a good story out of it? Perhaps you could follow various groups of people:

- The geologists who discover the increased gravity, investigate the cause, give warnings of the planet's impending collapse, try to prevent it, and so on. Their warnings will be ignored initially, of course.

- The rescue workers digging people out of the collapsed buildings that result from the growing number of earthquakes.

- Some ordinary families. Show how their lives are affected. Some of them might be the families of the geologists or rescue workers.

- Space scientists who are trying to find ways of deflecting and diverting the asteroids and comets.

- And so on.

What caused the gravity to increase and the planet to shrink? Could it have been prevented? Were warning signs missed? Is a happy ending even possible?

51. Own the Moon

Inspire yourself to write better Moon-based stories by owning a piece of it. You could set all of your Moon stories on your own personal plot of Moon land.

You can buy an acre (or more) of the Moon from MoonEstates.com. They also sell land on Venus and Mars.

It's unlikely that you'll ever get to visit your piece of Moon land in real life, of course. But in fiction you can do whatever you like with it:

- build on it

- dig for minerals

- use it as a launch base for other missions

- invade other people's Moon territory

- and whatever else you can think of

52. Parallel universes

Many science fiction stories discuss the existence of parallel universes, or even take place in them.

Some scientists believe that parallel universes are real. But they probably don't mean the science fiction version of them, in which every eventuality leads to a whole new parallel universe.

For example, let's say that you bought a lottery ticket, but you didn't win. Science Fiction's Law of Parallel Universes dictates that in another universe, you *did* win. The act of buying the losing ticket, or seeing the result of the lottery draw, created a new universe in which your ticket was the winning one.

You might think that if you could find that other universe, and jump across to it, you'd instantly be rich. But, of course, things aren't as simple as that.

In theory, there must be an almost infinite number of parallel universes: and in most of them, you won't exist.

Consider the odds of you being born: they're incredibly tiny. Your parents both had to be born on this planet - and there might be billions of inhabited planets in each universe. Then they had to meet and fall in love. And then they had to stay together long enough to have children. They had to have sexual intercourse at exactly the right time, during the exact month that your egg was released from your mother's ovaries. And so on. The chances of each of these things happening is incredibly small. In the vast majority of the parallel universes, none of those things happened, so you won't be there. Even in the universes where *most* of those things happened, if just one step in the chain didn't happen, you weren't born.

Even if you were born in some of those universes, you might not be there now. Do you remember when that car nearly hit you when you were a kid? In at least one of those universes, it *did* hit you, and you died. You might have had hundreds of narrow escapes like that during your lifetime. And that means there must be hundreds of other universes where you didn't escape, and you didn't survive.

Those universes won't be of any use to you. But how would you even begin to identify which ones you're alive and present in, let alone which one you won the lottery in?

Let's say you've found a way of identifying the right universe, and that you've also found a way of traveling to it – because there must be a parallel universe where that actually happens. Perhaps you have a handheld device that can do all of the calculations and take you there. How did you get this device?

So now you're in the parallel universe where you won the lottery.

But that doesn't mean *you* won the lottery. The *other you* that lives in that universe won the lottery. Not you. So, what's going to happen now that you're there too? There are two of you in the same universe. That (presumably) goes against the law of nature.

Will you kill him and take over his life?

Or will he attack you, take your device, and hop back over to your universe – with all of his winnings. Now he can take over your old life, and be rich, while you're stuck in his universe with nothing. Do they have the universe-hopping device there? If not, you're stranded – possibly forever.

Or will something else happen?

53. Patent records

It's easy to search through old patent records online. Google Patent Search (https://patents.google.com) is a good place to start, and I've also found Wikipedia (www.wikipedia.org) useful.

When you do this, you'll often come across all sorts of weird and wonderful inventions that were never actually built. These can provide you with an almost endless supply of story ideas. You'll also find gadgets, vehicles, weapons, medical equipment, labor-saving devices, kitchen utensils, new types of fuel and power-generation, and just about everything else you can imagine – as well as plenty that you can't.

54. Phenomena explained by science

Imagine that you could project yourself into the far future. What might science have found rational explanations for?

You could begin by thinking about phenomena that are currently beyond the realms of science. Yet they still have large numbers of believers and followers. There might also be plenty of credible witnesses and compelling evidence, even though our current science can't prove its validity.

For example, there might come a time when the existence of ghosts is proven. Or, on the other hand, they might be definitively proven *not* to exist.

Assuming they're proven to exist, that could lead to further developments. Perhaps there's a race to develop equipment that allows us to communicate with them easily. The ability to communicate freely with the spirit world will undoubtedly have other consequences. For example, the spirits of murder victims will be able to identify their killers, and perhaps also testify in court.

Proving that ghosts exist would also prove there's life after death.

What else might science be able to prove, explain, or account for? How about things like magic, witchcraft, the occult, Earth energies, dowsing, UFOs, aliens and other supernatural phenomena? What about the various religions and their assorted deities, artifacts, and legends?

If one or more of those could be proven (or disproven) the consequences are unimaginable. Well, not *quite* unimaginable, because you can use your imagination and tell the story of what happens.

[EXTENSION 1] It's worth looking at – and writing about – the things that were considered unexplained phenomena in the past, but have now been explained and proven (or disproven) by science.

[EXTENSION 2] You might like to consider whether, in proving or disproving these things, the scientists were telling the truth. Or could the government have ordered them to provide a plausible explanation for some other reason? Perhaps they were ordered to cover something up, to make the government look competent, to stop the public from looking too closely at what was really going on, or to demonstrate that people's tax dollars were being well spent. Has it *really* been proven or disproven?

55. Philosophy

Studying philosophy is a worthwhile pursuit for any writer, but especially for science fiction writers. It teaches you to question things that most people take for granted, and to see the possibilities that others miss.

Searching online for the phrase "philosophical questions" will bring up all sorts of ideas for stories, and all manner of topics you can explore further.

A good starting point is the book *Philosophy: The Basics* by Nigel Warburton.

56. Preventing transport disasters

Each year there are thousands of accidents and disasters involving various types of transport. Future generations will undoubtedly find a solution to these. But what might these solutions be? Self-driving cars should – in theory – lead to a significant reduction in traffic collisions. But how would you stop planes from crashing, prevent terrorism, prevent spacecraft disasters, stop train crashes and derailments, prevent ships from capsizing, and so on? Or, if you can't prevent these things, could you at least stop the people involved in them from getting seriously hurt or killed?

It's well worth keeping an eye on the news and looking out for stories about transport accidents and disasters. Follow the investigation all the way through to find out what exactly what went wrong. Then try to fix it (in your fictional world) so that the problem can never happen again.

You might like to concentrate on one particular mode of transport. For example, you could write about a brilliant engineer who gradually modifies and improves a particular form of transport throughout his life until it's as safe as he can possibly make it. And perhaps he then hands over the development to his successor.

Choosing his successor might make a great story in its own right. Will he choose one of his children, or an employee, or hold a competition, or do something else?

Of course, if you're going to turn this idea into a great story, things will need to go badly wrong. So what might happen? He might make things much worse before they get better. But how could that happen if he's so brilliant? Someone – perhaps a disgruntled rival – might sabotage the launch of his new vehicle. A manufacturer might inadvertently –

or deliberately – supply him with defective components in an effort to save money. And so on.

See how many ideas you can come up with to add tension to your story and have your readers on the edges of their seats. You need to make them anxious to find out what happens next and how it all works out.

57. Raised by robots

There have been a few real-life cases of lost, abandoned or orphaned babies being brought up by monkeys, dogs, wolves, and other wild animals. But what if a baby was brought up by robots?

Would he grow up thinking he's a robot too? What will he do when he finds out he's human? How do the robots manage to bring him up without other humans being aware that they're doing it? Why would they do that rather than hand him back to the humans? Do they think he's a robot?

What will the robots teach him about humans? Are they enemies? Do they regard them as superior or inferior? Or do they not have those kinds of feelings?

What if humans find or capture the baby? Will the humans think he's a robot too? What might they do to him? What if they discover that he's human? Will they have to teach him how to be human? Or will it be instinctive once he's with his own kind? The robots might even have given him several advantages over other humans.

At what point do the humans discover he's human? Is it when they try to take him apart? Or when he cries? Or when he does something that no robot would ever do?

Or perhaps they never find out he's human. And perhaps the baby never finds out he's human.

> [EXTENSION] What if the robots are evil? What if they're trying to take over the world and enslave the humans? Why would they bring up the baby so well rather than enslaving him? Will the humans think more kindly of the robots for doing that? Perhaps it might lead to a truce, and a promise not to destroy each other. Even if the humans still think the robots are evil – and vice versa.

58. Reversing time

Reversed-time stories are hugely popular with readers, and terrific fun to write.

Historical events take on new meaning when seen in reverse, and that can help readers understand them more clearly and profoundly.

Let's consider the death of Diana, Princess of Wales as an example.

In the reversed-time version, the dead princess is driven by ambulance from a French hospital to a road tunnel, where her body is placed in a wrecked car. The car is then driven at high speed by a (possibly) drunk driver to a hotel, by which time the princess has come back to life. During the journey to the hotel, the driver chases members of the paparazzi. The princess steps out of the car fully recovered and walks into the hotel, where she's given a good meal. But what happens to her next?

You could go through her whole life story: divorcing a prince, marrying him, going to work in a kindergarten, and so on. You might already know enough about her life to be able to extend this story and add more detail. Since some of the facts aren't known, there's also room for your own interpretation, as well as other people's opinions, conspiracy theories, and speculation. But all in reverse, of course.

Or you could write about something else. Your story might include things such as:

- wounds that slowly open up and then heal themselves in an instant

- rotten food that becomes fresh again

- meat that turns back into living animals

- fruit growing on a tree, and the tree gradually reabsorbs it

- clouds that pull rain out of the ground and suck it up into the air

- rivers that flow uphill

- logs and coal are created by fire

- cutting grass makes it longer

- and so on

It's probably best not to mention what happens at mealtimes. Or what happens in restrooms.

How about an artist? His job might involve buying paintings, carefully removing the paint one brushstroke at a time, then selling the blank canvas and tubes of paint to an art supply store.

A sculptor might buy statues that people no longer want, take them back to his studio, and hammer stone chips onto them to create a solid block of rock. He might sell these blocks to a quarry, where they're used to fill in all the holes in the landscape.

What exactly do writers do? And why do they claim it's such hard work?

What do teachers do?

Do any jobs stay exactly the same?

Once you start thinking about all the things that might happen in a reversed-time world, the possibilities are endless.

59. Robot crime

What if a robot committed a crime? There might even be a gang of rogue robots. That should make a great story. Perhaps one or more of the police officers or private detectives involved in the case is a robot too. And how about a robot dog to help track down the villains?

Why has the robot gone rogue? What is its motivation?

Has someone deliberately programmed it to commit crimes? If so, who did it? How can the investigators trace the human culprits?

Imagine trying to interview robot suspects and robot witnesses. How would you extract a confession? Would it involve torture? Would the robot care about being tortured if it can obtain replacement parts easily? Can it even care at all? Can it feel pain? Does it realize it's committed a crime? Or does it believe it's completed its list of instructions as requested, and can't distinguish between right and wrong?

For example, if it's been instructed to enter an art gallery, locate a particular painting, remove it, and return it to the thief, is it guilty if it follows those instructions? Is it capable of conscious thought? Or does the robot in your story make the decision to take the painting all by itself, and no human is instructing it? What other crimes might it commit?

What might the robot do to avoid being caught? It might emit a jamming signal to block police radios and CCTV cameras. What if it's been programmed to self-destruct if it's cornered. How can the police arrest it or trace its human programmer in that case?

What might give it away? If it can broadcast jamming signals, perhaps something could detect those signals and reveal its location.

As you play around with this idea, you should be able to come up with all sorts of other ideas, interesting scenarios, and "what ifs."

60. Science fiction categories

Science fiction and fantasy readers often divide themselves into distinct factions, preferring a certain category of science fiction and nothing else. They generally have a core group of authors whom they love – and they read everything they write. Many of them hate the other categories, factions, and authors with a passion.

Those who don't express their hatred for the other categories will totally ignore them. You'll be wasting your time if you try to target those readers. You'll also be in trouble if something on your cover or in your title or sub-title implies that your story belongs in their category when it actually belongs in a different one. You'll probably end up with one-star reviews if any of them read your work, regardless of how good it is.

So, before you start writing science fiction, you need to decide exactly which category of it you're going to write. The easiest way of doing this is to find other writers whose work is similar to the sort of thing you want to write. You probably read their books already.

It should be quite easy to work out which category of science fiction they write in, if you aren't sure. If they have an entry on Wikipedia, that will probably tell you. Their category listings on Amazon will also tell you. And it's worth looking them up on sites like Goodreads too, as both Amazon and Goodreads will lead you to other writers in the same category.

[TIP] Yasiv.com is another great site that shows the links and connections between books, authors and categories.

Once you know the category, you can dig deeper into it. Read books by other writers in that category. Search for the category online and learn about all the conventions and tropes that readers expect – and demand – in each story.

It's worth reading the reviews on Amazon and Goodreads too. These will tell you what readers like and dislike, what they hate to see, what makes a good story for them, and what ruins it.

The reviews – along with comments posted on websites, forums and in Facebook groups dedicated to that category – might also suggest ideas for stories readers would like to see but which haven't been written yet. You might also find predictions about the future, ideas for new gadgets and inventions, and all sorts of other things. They're a goldmine for science fiction writers.

[NOTE] Beware of joining in the discussions on some of these websites if you're brand new to the category. Some of the long-term contributors can be a little obsessive and aggressive. I would hang around in the background and read what everyone is saying for a few weeks before joining in. You might even decide not to join in at all: just read their comments and suggestions, and use them.

61. Social commentary

You can use science fiction to comment on various aspects of our own lifestyles. For example, if you oppose the genetic modification of food crops, you could write about what happened when another planet tried it. In your story, it will of course go tragically wrong.

Similarly, you could look at – and comment upon – such things as:

- inter-species organ transplants

- life after death

- religion

- cloning

- the occult and the paranormal

- entertainment and celebrity culture

- politics

- war

- business

- finance

- crime and punishment

- diseases and disabilities and their treatments

- the use and abuse of drugs

- education

- as well as hundreds of other aspects of our modern lives

If you feel particularly strongly about one of these issues, write a story that warns what might happen if we continue along our current path.

A good science fiction story can make your point far more effectively than a strongly worded letter to a newspaper. And the pay can be much better too.

[EXTENSION 1] In the list above I suggested various aspects of our modern lives. But you don't have to restrict yourself to the present when looking for ideas.

What issues did we face in the past that might have been handled differently on other planets?

What issues will we face in the future? How did they work out on other planets?

Again, you'll suggest in your story that when other planets tried it, it all went horribly wrong.

[EXTENSION 2] Will you also offer a solution – a right way of doing things that will work out well for us?

62. Social commentary – built-in obsolescence

There was a time when products were built to last. Sadly, that's not the case any more. These days the accountants are in charge, and they want everyone to buy replacement products every couple of years, not keep them for decades or hand them down to their children as family heirlooms, as we once did. As a result, products are deliberately designed to fail, or go out of fashion or become obsolete. It's hardly ethical, of course, but it's the world we live in now. But where will it all lead? Will we continue to accept this practice? That's something you could explore in a story.

For example, what might happen when our homes are entirely controlled by technology? Will they keep going wrong? Will every home need a repair engineer on permanent standby?

And what will happen to the ever-growing mountain of faulty, unrepairable things? Will they be dumped on an unsuspecting planet or moon? Or recycled? Will the householders of tomorrow need an infinite budget just to stay alive? Or will there be "extended warranties" to take care of all that? And will those extended warranties be as much of a rip-off as they are today?

[EXTENSION] What about compatibility issues between similar products purchased on other planets? For example, will you still be able to watch a movie you bought on Proxima Centauri 7 when you get back to Earth? Probably not. Well, perhaps not legally. But there might be a software patch available on the internet that'll get around it. But why should it be illegal anyway, since you paid for the movie in the first place?

What else might you be able to fix with illegal patches? What could you avoid paying for?

What else might be compatible or incompatible on different planets, or on different parts of the same planet?

63. Social commentary – outsourcing

Many companies outsource work to countries where labor is cheaper. Their staff don't like it, and nor do their customers, especially when they outsource customer service roles. This practice has been in the news for years now. Some companies have begun to realize that people don't like it, and they're pulling the outsourced roles back to their own countries. It's been fascinating to watch this unfold, and you might like to comment on it in the form of a story.

Imagine that the practice was tried centuries ago on another planet. Did it succeed? Probably not. But did it fail there for the same reasons as it seems to have failed on Earth – because customers want to deal with people from their own culture and who speak their language? Or was there a different issue on the other planet? What advice might someone on that planet give to companies on Earth that are thinking of trying this? How would you turn that into the underlying idea for your story, while still making it a compelling read?

Perhaps the bosses in your story outsource work to other planets. Or perhaps alien immigrants are willing to come to the bosses' planet and do the native workers' jobs for a fraction of the price. How well will that work out? What might go wrong? Won't the native workers rebel?

And who is left to do the work on the immigrants' planet? Will they have to cut services and close companies because they no longer have enough staff? Could they offer higher wages, or is that not possible in their economy? Will the entire planet end up being abandoned because there's no one left to run the everyday services people need? There are plenty of things that could go horribly wrong. And that makes for a great story.

Perhaps you could write about a future Earth where the countries or planets we outsourced all our work to have become rich industrial giants, while the native workers are out of work and broke. Is there a solution to this crisis?

Perhaps in your story about the future Earth, the unemployed native workers abandon their own countries and move their families to the rich industrial giants. Places like India, China, and the Philippines might have plenty of work, high wages, and a fantastic standard of living. Places like the USA, UK and parts of Western Europe might become empty wastelands. Who would stay behind – or get left behind? How would they survive with no money, no goods and services, and possibly no government?

Is there a solution to this crisis? What did the other planets do to get their citizens to come home? How did they become wealthy again? Or did no one ever return?

64. Space TV

How about taking existing Earth-based TV shows and moving them into space?

- Perhaps you could have a gardening show set on Mars. It might feature both the inside and the outside of the dome that people live in.

- Or how about an interior design show for people living on a space station?

- Or a show that follows veterinarians who care for space creatures?

- And so on.

You'll get plenty of ideas from just watching TV or studying the TV listings guide. Think about how you might be able to adapt each show to work in a space environment or on another planet. Could you turn it into a story? Or would it make an interesting or amusing scene or background detail in your novel or screenplay?

The making of the show, and the numerous problems the crew has to deal with, could make up your entire story. There's plenty of scope for a series of stories if you do that.

65. Start with a soap opera

TV soap operas can be a terrific source of science fiction ideas. Seriously!

Pick a soap, study a few episodes, and get to know the characters. You'll probably be able to find guides online that explain who's who and what has happened to them in the past. Many of the characters will be related to each other, or will have had relationships with several of the other characters. They might have secrets that some characters know about and some don't. TV viewers might not know all of the secrets yet, but they probably suspect a few things. They might be aware that something is lurking in a particular character's background just waiting to be revealed.

Then you have the typical everyday soap opera storylines: murder, rape, kidnapping, carjacking, incest, robbery, fires – both deliberate and accidental, adultery, bigamy, blackmail, threats of violence, immoral business dealing, gambling, addictions, mental health issues, accidents, injuries, deaths, births, marriages, jiltings, troublemakers, terrible neighbors, backstabbing, bad decisions, all the complicated family problems and inter-relationships, and much more.

All you have to do then is take the characters and storylines and stick them on a spacecraft. You immediately have a science fiction story with a wonderful sense of everyday realism, a whole heap of problems, and everlasting series potential.

They don't have to be living on a spaceship, of course.

- They might live on another planet, perhaps under a city-sized perspex dome.

- They might be scattered over several planets or colonies.

- They might live in different dimensions or times.

- Or it could be something else – the science fiction aspect of the story is entirely up to you.

If you start off with the soap opera and then add the science fiction aspect, you'll create a level of realism that's rarely seen in this genre. Most science fiction writers start off with the science fiction aspect and then add the characters and storyline.

Of course, you can't just purloin someone else's soap opera. You can use one as a basis for your story, but you'll need to change the characters' names at the very least. But if you've always wanted to have a go at writing your own soap opera, this could be the perfect opportunity. Or you could do it the easy way and base your soap opera on an existing one.

[TIP] You'll find more ideas on writing soap operas in our Screenplays and Fiction ideas collections.

[NOTE] George Lucas used this idea when he created *Star Wars*. And it certainly worked well for him.

66. Super-long-distance communication

Let's imagine that we've made contact with intelligent beings on another planet. Let's say it's 75 light years away. Obviously, it makes no sense for us to send them a message, wait 75 years for it to reach them, and then wait another 75 years for their reply. Instead, once we've established that they can understand us and we can understand them, each planet might send a continual stream of questions, answers and other data.

But how many questions and how much data should they send? One per day? Or ten? Or a hundred? Should it be more than that? Should it be thousands? Who decides what each day's questions, answers and data will be?

Perhaps your story is set 75 years in the future, and the first set of questions from the other planet is about to arrive. Do we know they're coming? If so, how do we know? Did they send an advance notice a month before their transmissions would begin? Did anyone receive the advance notice? Did they repeat the message daily? Did anyone receive it? How did they know we were here to receive their messages?

Someone needs to be ready to receive them, record them, find out the answers if necessary, and send a reply. But will anyone be ready? The data might be picked up by an amateur astronomer or radio operator. Will he be the main character in your story? Or is he a minor character to relays the data to your main character and his team?

[NOTE] To avoid any confusion, the questions will either need to be numbered, or the original question will need to be sent back to them along with our reply.

Or perhaps your story is set 150 years in the future and the answers to the first set of questions we asked 150 years ago are just about to start coming back from the other planet.

What will they say? Will their answers be helpful? Will we like what they tell us? Is their civilization more or less advanced than ours? What advice can they offer us? Do they need our help? Or do we need theirs?

Could we exchange other things apart from questions and simple data? How images, video, audio, drawings, books, plans, schematic diagrams, chemical and molecular formulas, sections of our genome, and so on?

67. Technology – use and misuse

Many science fiction stories are concerned with the use – or, more likely, the misuse – of a new invention. This usually involves a character or organization doing something with the technology that its inventor never intended. But you don't need to restrict yourself to new inventions. There are plenty of old or current technologies that you could find alternative uses for – especially if you're a cunning and enterprising space villain.

Perhaps your villain has a particular crime in mind, and he's looking for a tool that will help him accomplish it. Or maybe he comes across the invention first, and then realizes that it might have potential as a criminal tool, so he builds his crime around it.

It doesn't have to be used for a criminal purpose, of course. Perhaps the crew of your spacecraft is in trouble, and they need a specific tool that they don't have. Why don't they have it? Has it been lost or stolen or broken? Describe what happened. Since they don't have that tool, they'll have to use whatever is available.

What have you got lying around your home that could be adapted for a purpose no one has thought of yet?

What was the most recent piece of electronic equipment you bought? Could it be adapted into a new type of weapon? Could it be used to commit a crime – on Earth or on a spacecraft or on another planet? Could it be used for espionage? Could you add an extra "hidden" feature and turn it into a James Bond-style gadget?

It needn't even be an object. There are all sorts of other discoveries, scientific laws and principles, mathematical formulas, and so on just waiting to be used, abused, rediscovered, and pressed into service in new and imaginative ways. See what you can come up with.

68. Teleportation – implications

One day, in the far, far distant future, it might be possible for us to teleport ourselves to wherever we want to go without all the hassle of traveling there. Aside from the ease and speed of getting around, how else might our lives be affected by this? It's well worth thinking about because you should be able to get hundreds of stories out of it.

You could start by asking a few questions:

- What will happen to the roads and railway lines, the car industry and all the other industries associated with it, oil-rich nations, fuel processors, airports and airport staff, car parks, taxis, buses, postal deliveries, and so on?

- Will everyone become obese because they no longer bother walking? Will exercise be made compulsory?

- What if two people rematerialized in the same spot at exactly the same time? Or can something be done to prevent that from ever happening? What if everyone in the world decided to go to the same place at the same time, and there was nothing to stop them?

- What about customs and border controls? They might cease to exist. In fact, international borders might cease to exist. Would the whole world become a single country?

- Smuggling might become extremely easy, and there might be no way of keeping illegal immigrants and asylum seekers out. But if there was only one country and only one world government that might not matter. If we were all citizens of the same country, there'd be no such thing as immigration.

- Would access to the teleportation technology be restricted? Would it be cheap or free or prohibitively expensive? Who could afford it?

- Could it be accessed on the black market?

- Some people say that "getting there is half the fun." If getting there was eliminated, would we only be half as happy? Or would we be twice as happy because of the time saving and convenience?

- How far does the teleportation system reach? Could we use it to launch satellites and spacecraft? Or beam ourselves to other planets and moons without the need for spacecraft? How would we get back again? Could we teleport an entire teleportation system or the components to build one?

The more you think about it, the more our lives would change beyond all recognition. Keep thinking about it for a few more days, and see how far you can extend the list of questions above. You'll end up with some fantastic ideas for stories, scenes, characters, settings, jobs, and other background details.

69. *The Encyclopedia of Science Fiction*

The Encyclopedia of Science Fiction (http://mybook.to/sfpedia) is a terrific time-saver for writers. If you want to write about a time machine, for example, just look up "time machine." The encyclopedia will tell you when the concept was first used in fiction and what twists and additions other writers have made since then. (Or at least up until 1999 when the book was released.) That saves you from having to track down and read every time machine story that's ever been published. You can base your story on one of those ideas, try to extend it in a new direction, or try to come up with an original time travel idea that hasn't been used yet. At least you'll know which ones have already been done.

Or you could simply browse through the encyclopedia and consider all the possibilities. You could use it for inspiration and see what occurs to you. Or you could adapt and extend what other writers have done, find new angles, and so on. It's a massive book, and with over 4,300 entries and 1,400 pages, you won't run out of ideas any time soon.

> **[NOTE]** At the time of writing, I could find no recent books on the market that cover the subject in such depth. If you're a true science fiction fan and you fancy taking on a mammoth project, perhaps you could extend the encyclopedia and bring it up to date. It might be too much work for just one person, so perhaps you could work on it with a group of like-minded friends.

70. The future of reading groups

Imagine what a reading group or book club of the future might be like, and then write a story about it.

What if you haven't had time to read the book? No problem: you can probably order it just by thinking about it and download it straight into your brain.

There might be an "instant know-it-all" edition too, which analyses the book in excruciating detail and explains all the theories behind it. Perfect if you want to be the nerd of the group and you haven't read it. Of course, it'll cost you a little more. The literary analysis was almost certainly done by a computer, of course.

What if you can't attend this month's book club meeting? No problem: you could attend it in virtual reality instead. Or send a hologram or a robot to represent you. It'll look like you and have your voice and brain pattern. Perhaps no one will know the difference.

What if you don't like the other members of the group? No problem: just switch your brain augmentation chip to "altered perception" mode. Instantly, they all look like movie stars, and their personalities will seem so much nicer.

What other ideas can you come up with?

Don't forget to include some conflict in your story – we don't want everyone to have it too easy. What if the members disagree about the book they're supposed to have read? What if the disagreement gets out of hand?

What else might go wrong? What else do they talk or argue about apart from the books? What's going on in their lives outside the book club?

Can the other members help? Perhaps they read something in one of their books that might help. But dare they try it?

[EXTENSION] What if the members of the group are the leaders of various countries, and the disagreement leads to war?

Or they might be leaders of something else – major companies for example – and it might lead to trouble of a different sort.

71. The laws and theories of science

As far as I know, this doesn't exist yet. I'd really like to see a book or website that lists all the different laws and theories of science, mathematics, space and time. It would summarize each of them in a single paragraph of plain English. This would be a fantastic tool that would make it really easy to come up with science fiction ideas.

Please could someone create this! But check that it doesn't exist already – perhaps under a strange or obscure name. If it exists, perhaps you could help to popularize it, or give it a better name. If it's a website, perhaps you could work with the creator to turn it into a book.

Assuming it doesn't exist, you could start collecting as many laws and theories as you can find, write short summaries of them, and compile them into a book or website of your own. Perhaps you could start with a website or blog first, and then turn it into a book when you have enough.

You could list a few of the laws and theories you already know about on the website, and invite people to submit more or improve your summaries. That way, you'll build up a huge collection of them without having to do too much work. You'll also be doing the science fiction world a huge favor.

72. The laws and theories of science – getting rid of

Scientific laws are all well and good, but sometimes they get in the way of telling a good story. So let's get rid of them, or change them to work the way we'd really like them to.

[NOTE] You might have to set your story in a different universe to make this idea sound plausible.

Let's consider friction. How about writing a story set in a world where there isn't any friction? That should be pretty interesting. How the heck will anything work?

And how about writing another story where friction works in reverse? For example, if you kick a ball, it won't ever slow down; it'll keep getting faster and faster until it hits something – or someone. By that point, it might be traveling faster than a bullet. It could cause serious damage or even kill someone.

There are plenty of other laws you could experiment with: gravity, the speed of sound, the speed of light, electrical conductance and resistance, and all sorts of others. Choose one – or more than one if you like – and remove it, reverse it, or alter it in some other way. Think about what the effect would be. If you think it would make a good basis for a story, write it.

Of course, trying to write a story about how everything in the world would be affected by this would be an impossible task. It might be better to focus on just one aspect and build your story around that.

For example, you could write about a bank robbery that takes place in that world. You could follow the build-up, the planning, the execution, the arrests, trial and imprisonment. Maybe even a prison escape.

But how would each aspect of the story differ from the bank robbery stories we're more familiar with?

You need to keep in mind that changing just one of the fundamental laws of physics will have a profound effect on every aspect of your characters' lives.

If there's no friction, the cars in your world won't have any brakes. That might mean there are no cars. In fact, how can people even stand up and walk around? They won't be able to get a grip on the floor. Perhaps someone invents Velcro for this very purpose. In fact, it might have been invented hundreds of thousands of years ago in your world. What might it have evolved into by now?

Perhaps people move around in much the same way as they do on spacecraft in orbit. They push themselves off of one surface and slide across the floor until they bump into something else. There might be lots of closely spaced, well-padded walls, each with plenty of things to grip on to.

Picking things up will be tricky too. With no friction, won't everything slip out of your fingers? Would it even be possible to live in this weird universe? Doesn't the body need friction to be able to function? You'll need to come up with some clever ideas to make it work, but it'll be a fascinating story.

73. The Science Museum – and others like it

If you're interested in writing science fiction and you're in the UK, a visit to the Science Museum in London is a must.

Ideally, plan to spend at least two days there. Spend the first day wandering around and enjoying all the exhibits – it will take you an entire day to see everything. Then spend the second day taking a closer look at specific things you could write about. Think about how you might incorporate them into a story, or build a story around them.

Think about what each piece of technology might lead to in the future. Look at how primitive the technology from just forty or fifty years ago seems now. Some of the medical machinery from that era looks absolutely lethal. How primitive will today's technology appear in forty or fifty years, and what will take its place? What about even further into the future?

There are lots of other science and technology museums, exhibitions and collections elsewhere in the UK and all around the world. There should be one within a reasonable traveling distance of where you live.

The Science Museum has something for everyone, so it's a great place to visit if you're searching around for ideas for things to write about.

But if you want to write about a particular topic, such as space travel or computing or medicine, there are museums, exhibitions, and collections elsewhere that cater specifically for those things. They'll have many more items in their collections that will interest you.

To find one that's close to you, search online for the topic that interests you, plus the word "museum" or "collection" and the name of your country or state. For example: computer museum New York.

74. Time bomb

Some words and phrases have very different meanings if you take them literally. A good example is "time bomb." The dictionary definition is: "a bomb designed to explode at a certain time" or "something that threatens to have an abruptly disastrous outcome in the future." But never mind what the dictionary says; what do you think a *literal* time bomb might do?

It could, for example, be a next-generation weapon. It doesn't kill; it doesn't injure; it just blasts your victim(s) into the middle of next week. (Or last week, or last month or even last year if you use a powerful enough bomb.) Your victims might not even realize anything has happened to them. In fact, they might think it was *you* that vanished.

What might happen if a war was fought using time bombs? What if one side has them and the other side doesn't? Perhaps the side that has them could blast the enemy several days into the past and then set traps for them, or ambush them with conventional weapons when they eventually make it back to wherever they disappeared from. The whole direction of the war would change instantly.

What if the side that was losing deployed time bombs instead of retreating?

75. Time travel 1

Scientists in science fiction stories often build time machines and attempt to go back in time and stop something from happening. But Mother Nature doesn't like history being interfered with, and she'll undoubtedly find a different way of achieving the same outcome. This can make for a compelling and intriguing story with countless variations. Here are some examples:

Our hero goes back in time to prevent the birth of a brutal dictator. A brutal dictator is born anyway. He just happens to be a *different* brutal dictator this time around. Our hero has fixed the wrong problem.

Perhaps he should have gotten rid of the regime, not the person leading it.

Our hero goes back in time to prevent a child from being killed, but the child is killed by something else instead. Our hero might make repeated attempts to save the child, but the child dies for a different reason every time. Will he ever manage to save the child? And if he does, does that mean another child will die instead?

Our hero sees the winning numbers for this week's lottery and goes back in time to buy his ticket. But when this week's numbers are drawn, they aren't the ones he expected.

Our hero goes back in time to prevent an incident that led to the outbreak of war. But the war breaks out anyway. Something else caused it this time around.

Almost bankrupt, our hero revisits the key turning points in his life and takes the opposite decision or pathway. But each time he returns to the present day, he always ends up penniless.

See how many more ideas like these you can come up with. You should be able to turn them into fantastic stories. And, of course, if you can't think of any of your own, you could always use one of the ideas above.

76. Time travel 2

What if someone from the past time-traveled to the present day to meet you? And what if that person was you in a previous life? Perhaps he wanted to find out what happened to his spirit after he died, and his search through time led him to you. He insists that you both share the same spirit, but how can he prove it to you?

How would you feel about it? Would you turn him away? Or would you welcome him and take him on a tour of the modern world? Could he take you back to his time so you could see one of your previous lives? Why couldn't he just hypnotize you and perform a past-life regression to save all that tricky time-traveling? Perhaps past-life regression wasn't known about in his time, and he doesn't know it's possible.

Was he the first incarnation of your spirit, or were there others before him? If there were others, perhaps you could both go and visit them too. And you could visit your future incarnations too. In fact, you could try visiting everyone in your entire "spirit chain." Where and when did your spirit begin? How, why, and when does it end – if it ever does? You could easily turn this into a series, looking at one of your lifetimes in each story.

As you meet each of your previous incarnations, perhaps they could join you on your journey. You'll be an ever-growing band of time-travelers who all look different but are spiritually the same person.

Perhaps your spirit eventually reaches Nirvana and no longer reincarnates. Perhaps your spirit is obliterated in a dreadful accident or attack by a demon. Or perhaps something else happens. How will you and your fellow time-travelers feel when you reach the end of your journey and learn your ultimate fate?

You could invent the character in this story, and invent each of his past and future incarnations. Or you could base the character on you. Or you could try having some actual past-life regression sessions and see if they lead to anything you could write about. You'll still have to invent the future ones, of course. Or perhaps, when you're thinking deeply about this topic, you might meet your future incarnations in a series of dreams. That would be useful!

[TIP] You should be able to declare your past-life regression sessions as a business expense when filing your tax return.

77. Time travel 3

What if our planet was headed for disaster? Relocating everyone to a new planet might be impractical or even impossible. But what if we could send the entire population forward or backward through time to a place of safety?

It's a great idea for a story, but you'll need to answer a lot of questions before you write it:

Who invents the time machine and how? Was it a lone inventor working in his garage, or a government-funded research institute? Could it have been reverse-engineered from an alien spacecraft – even if the government won't admit that's what happened?

Who is the first person to try it? How far does he travel? How does he get back to the present day to tell us whether the machine is safe to use?

Who goes on a reconnaissance mission to find a safe time to live in? Do they go forward or backward in time? Presumably, at least one person will travel forward to find out whether the Earth avoids or survives the impending disaster. Does it survive? Does the heroic time-traveler survive?

Once a safe place is found, who makes the decision to send everyone through the machine? Is it voluntary or compulsory? What if some people refuse to go? How long have they got before disaster strikes?

We might need thousands of time machines to send the entire population to their new time. How many people can each machine handle? Who builds them? What happens if some of the machines break down? What if someone sabotages them? A religious or doomsday cult might try to destroy them.

Do the machines operate automatically, or does someone have to stay behind to operate them? Perhaps those who refuse to travel through them can stay behind and operate them: so that's a problem solved!

What will people find when they arrive in their new time? What problems might they now have to face?

Let's assume they go back a few million years. They'll need to rebuild modern civilization, complete with governments, schools, hospitals, churches, food production and distribution, electricity, computers, and so on. How long will that take? Which of these things takes priority? Did they bring any tools and equipment through the time machine with them?

Are there any early hominins already living there? If there are, will the time-travelers wipe them out, or put them in zoos or reservations, or enslave them and make them build the new society? Or will they do something else?

What if everyone went to the future instead? Let's assume the Earth is severely affected by the disaster, but it eventually becomes habitable again. What sort of state will the time-travelers find it in when they arrive in the future? Will they have to rebuild everything from scratch, or did some of our current civilization and technology survive?

Perhaps there's already a modern society there, built by the descendants of those who stayed behind and somehow survived. But how could they have survived?

78. Time travel 4

What if time moves at different speeds at different points in history?

Our hero might travel to a different period but find that he isn't in sync with it.

He might appear to speak too quickly or too slowly, and no one can understand him.

His brain might operate much faster than other people's. He might be able to out-think and outwit even their smartest scientists.

On the other hand, if his brain operates more slowly than everyone else's, he might seem less intelligent than the village idiot.

If he moves more slowly than everyone else, he could be in grave danger. He might not be able to get away from things quickly enough; even crossing the street might be impossible.

But if he moves really quickly compared to everyone else, he could beat all of their speed records. Or perhaps everyone will treat him as some kind of freak – or worse. At least he should be fast enough to run away from danger.

[EXTENSION] You could also explore the situation where your hero returns to the present after spending years in the past or future. He might return to the present just minutes after he left, yet he will have aged considerably.

On the other hand, he might spend just a few minutes in the past or future, but when he tries to return to the present, something goes wrong. He might end up a few minutes too early and meet himself. Or he might end up month, years, decades or centuries off-course.

He might not even know where – or when – he is. He might have no way of getting back – perhaps his battery was running low and he could only make one time-jump. And now he's in a time or place where there's no electricity. He might have to get inventive and recharge his battery using lemons or potatoes – or something else.

But what if he can't return to his own time at all? That particular period of history might have been destroyed while he was away. Perhaps it was because of something he did while he was in the past. Or perhaps that period of history was – and is – perfectly fine, but the ability to reach it via time-travel was somehow destroyed. Will he ever get home?

79. Time travel 5

In most time travel stories the characters travel many years into the past or future. But in this story, our hero only jumps a few minutes.

Let's say he's trying to get a girl to agree to date him. She turns him down. He jumps a few minutes back in time and tries again – a different approach this time. She turns him down again. So he keeps jumping back again and again until he eventually finds something that works.

Of course, he'll have to jump back slightly further each time to avoid meeting himself. And when he eventually succeeds, he'll need to take the girl away from that spot as quickly as possible, otherwise she'll meet him multiple times.

He might use his time-traveling ability in other ways too. As before, whenever he comes up against a problem, he might jump back in time a few minutes and either avoid the problem altogether or try out different ways of solving it until he finds something that works.

A simple example would be if his boss asked him to stay late after work. If he jumps back a few minutes, he can make himself scarce when he hears his boss coming.

But if the technique works for simple issues like that, he should also be able to use it to solve much more complex problems – and even save the world.

You could also combine these two ideas into a single story. He might have to make lots of short jumps into the past to solve a really tricky problem. When he eventually solves it, he might be several hours in the past. But that means he's gone back to the time before the girl agreed to date him. So he has to try and win her all over again.

Of course, he knows what worked last time around when she agreed to date him. So it should work again this time ... shouldn't it? Well, yes, in theory. But if the circumstances have changed slightly, or his timing is off, she might say no.

80. Time travel alternatives

What if your villain is the time-traveler, rather than your hero?

The villain might come from a different era and end up in your hero's time. Do they know each other?

If the villain came from the past, your hero might know one of his descendants. Or, if the villain came from the future, your hero might know one of his ancestors.

Why is the villain a villain in your story? Does he have evil intentions? Does he want something that belongs to your hero? Or does it belong to someone your hero cares about and wants to protect? Or perhaps he doesn't care that much for it, but he's being paid to protect it and he wants to make sure he gets paid and maintains his good reputation.

What if your hero and your villain both end up in the same time period, but they each traveled there from different times? Your hero might have come from the past, while your villain might have come from the future. (Or it could be the other way around, of course.) Perhaps they both want the same thing, but only one of them can have it. How did they find out about it? How did they know where (and when) to come?

How will they cope in an era that's unfamiliar to them? They not only need to get the thing they came for, and stop the other person from getting it, they also have to:

- survive

- avoid getting arrested

- find their way around

- merge into the crowd and not stand out too much

- speak the local language

- and so on

If they're staying for a while, they might also need to find somewhere to sleep, buy food, ask people questions, and so on.

[EXTENSION 1] You could add a romantic element to your story. How will your bewildered hero get on with the ladies of this era?

If he's visiting the past, he might remember – or half-remember – things from history lessons and novels. But if he's visiting the future, he'll have nothing to go on. He'll just have to hope that basic human behavior and customs haven't changed too much.

[EXTENSION 2] The other characters in your story might have come from different time periods too. They've all ended up in the same place at the same time. But why?

- How did they get there, and how will they get home again?

- How long will they be staying for?

- How well will people from different eras adapt to this time period?

- Which of them finds it easiest to adapt, and which ones find it hardest?

- Are they all trying to get the same thing? Can only one of them get it? Or will they organize themselves into two teams, and one team will succeed and the other one won't?

- How seriously do they take this? Will the two teams be ferocious enemies and try to kill each other? Or is it all for fun? Will some of the participants switch sides if they think they'll stand a better chance of succeeding with the other team?

- Will some of them stay behind permanently at the end – either accidentally or deliberately?

- Will some of them make friends with people from another time and go and live with them instead, rather than returning to their own times?

- If they decide to stay, will they return to their own time to let everyone know they're not coming back? Or will they simply never return to the time they came from? What might happen to the people they left behind in their own eras? Will any of them come looking for them?

81. *Tomorrow's World* and other popular science shows

The BBC TV series *Tomorrow's World* has long since been discontinued, sadly. Many of us still remember it fondly. You might be able to find some old episodes – they're well worth watching. And, of course, there are plenty of other science and technology TV shows you could watch – though none of them quite the same as *Tomorrow's World*.

The closest equivalents in Britain today are *The Gadget Show* (Channel 5) and *Click* (BBC News).

The brilliant thing about *Tomorrow's World* was that it was so wide-ranging. It often featured prototypes of things that would never really take off. It was your one and only chance to see them.

But why wouldn't those things succeed? Were they simply not good enough? Was there no market for them? Did the government suppress them?

On the other hand, perhaps some of them are being used and developed right now. They might have been secretly adapted for military use. Perhaps foreign governments are using them against us without our knowledge.

It's worth following the progress of any discovery or invention that grabs your attention. If something seems to fail or disappear, think about what might have happened if it had succeeded, or what it might be being used secretly for today. Write an alternative history story in which it's in everyday use. Or write a story in which it's used for a more secretive purpose.

> **[EXTENSION]** It's also worth thinking about what might have become of the inventors of these things. If their product failed, did they try again with something else? Did it bankrupt them? Are they now working in dead-end jobs? Or did the government buy them out and make them rich? Are they now working for a secret underground organization – either officially or unofficially? Have they developed anything else since then?

82. Updating 1950s stories

Science fiction was enormously popular in the 1950s. Vast numbers of short stories were written, as well as novels. So why not look for collections of short stories from that period and see if any of them could be updated, or expanded into a novel?

The story will be protected by copyright, of course, so you'll need to credit the original author. If your work is accepted for publication, you'll need to let the editor or publisher know that it's based on someone else's story, and you might be asked to obtain permission. Usually, all that's needed is to add the words "Based on a story by ..."

Alternatively, you could change the story and the characters, so that they're no longer recognizable.

But the best thing to do would be to write a brand new story from scratch, and just use the original one for inspiration.

83. Using other people's stories 1

As well as writing science fiction, you probably read a lot of it too. And you've almost certainly come across at least one story that you disagreed with.

It might have suffered from one or more of the following common problems:

- The plot was unbelievable

- It had a terrible ending

- The idea was good, but it was badly written

- The idea was good, but you hated the characters

- History would never have followed that particular path

- People would never have reacted that way

- Government legislation would have prevented it

- The technology didn't make sense or was too far-fetched

- Or perhaps you thought there was something else wrong with it

Whatever problem you had with that story, here's your chance to fix it. Write a new version of the same story that follows the path you think it should have taken.

You could call it a rebuttal, or a refusal to accept the original author's idea. That would make an interesting marketing tactic. It will probably put you into conflict with the original author and his fans, and that could result in a significant amount of publicity for both of you.

On the other hand, perhaps you really liked the original story, but you think that taking the opposite angle, or an alternative one, would make a great story too. So go ahead and write it.

Science fiction writers borrow from each other all the time, so you shouldn't worry about doing this. It isn't "wrong." In fact, the original author will probably be flattered that you found his idea worthy of further examination.

If this sort of thing worries you at all, you should be able to find the author online. Ask him if he would agree to you writing new stories based on his ideas or set in his story world. Most authors will happily agree. And if they like your work, they might even offer to collaborate on some new ones.

84. Using other people's stories 2

Many science fiction stories mention intriguing facts, details, and inventions that the author came up with but didn't develop any further. They might be there to add color, or the author might have included them for his own amusement. But he might have decided not to explore them any further because they weren't particularly relevant to the story, or he might have run out of time or space.

That's where you come in. Whenever you come across a story like this that has interesting ideas but fails to fully explore or exploit them, take the time to explore them yourself. See if you can build a story around the idea or turn it into a component of a story: a character, a scene, a setting, a weapon, a gadget, or whatever it is.

[NOTE] Unless you have the other author's agreement, it's best to use these ideas as inspiration rather than using them directly.

Develop them into similar but slightly different things in your story, and give them different names.

It's also best to choose ideas from stories written by authors who are no longer writing. Contemporary authors might be planning to revisit their stories and develop those ideas themselves.

Of course, you could always contact the authors and ask if you could use them if they have no plans to use them themselves.

Most authors will agree to this, and they'll also be interested in seeing your finished work. They'll probably give you some tips and advice when they read it. That means you'll get free expert mentoring – and perhaps even gain a friend.

85. Westerns

Go to your local library and look at their selection of Westerns. See if you can find a great story about the early pioneers. Once you've found one, keep the plot and the characters' core functions and personalities, but change their names and move the whole thing into space.

Your story will probably include things like:

- finding a place for the new settlement

- the initial hardships and lack of facilities

- removing, resettling or killing the natives who object to their land being taken over

- fights and disputes between the settlers over various issues

Simply replace the settlers with space pioneers, the natives with aliens, and so on.

You should find that with a few tweaks and updates the story still works. Now all you have to do is write it: a fantastic new science fiction story with very little effort.

As it will all come together very quickly, you can afford to spend some extra time on other parts of the story. For example, you'll have time to work on the setting, dialogue, and description and make them really sparkle. And you might like to make the characters even more unique, realistic and intense than they were in the original story. They're in space now, so there are more things that could go wrong – and terrible consequences if they do. Everyone will be more anxious, tense, and alert than they would be on an open prairie. So turn their personalities up to eleven!

86. What might happen?

There are two ways of writing science fiction. One way is to write about what you think will happen in the future. The other way is to write about what *could* happen – but probably won't.

Aliens *probably won't* take control of the Earth within the next 100 years, so this won't be a future prediction story. But aliens *could* take control of the Earth within the next 100 years. It's plausible but highly unlikely – but it would still make a great story.

Let's explore that idea for a moment. Where might the aliens come from? How might they take over the Earth? Would it be an all-out war? Or would they establish colonies in quiet parts of the world and gradually spread outwards, over many years, conquering us as they go?

You could look at our real history for inspiration. For example, you could study the way the Romans conquered much of Europe 2000 years ago and introduced their own technology and culture. Just swap the Romans for aliens, and you'll hardly need to change anything else to tell a great story.

What else *might* happen – but probably won't – that futurologists wouldn't be able to predict?

- How about a robot uprising?

- What if humans became entirely digital entities?

- What if the Earth turned out to be an alien spacecraft?

- What if we were the aliens?

- What if we could travel many times faster than light?

- What if time travel became commonplace?

Once you start thinking about it, you should be able to come up with hundreds of other examples. If you get stuck, try discussing it with your friends; they'll probably have all sorts of interesting ideas.

87. What's in our water?

A recent news report said there are traces of anti-depressant drugs in our tap water. So many people are now taking these drugs that they're passing through them and ending up in our drinking water. But what if anti-depressants were being pumped into our water deliberately, just like fluoride is in many places?

The government might be surreptitiously raising the nation's mood to make us all more compliant and productive. Perhaps we'll also be more inclined to overlook their mistakes and crooked deals, and re-elect them. Maybe we'll be more supportive of higher taxes too.

We also know there are excessive levels of female hormones in our water. This is because so many women take contraceptive pills. The significant fall in male sperm counts in recent years has been attributed to this. The hormones are having strange effects on fish too.

The level of female hormones in our water will continue to rise unless something is done to stop it. And there's no sign of that happening. So where might it all end? Will every man become infertile, leading to the end of the human race? Is it reversible? Or is it already too late?

Perhaps the only way humanity can be saved is if we drink from pure, uncontaminated mountain springs rather than recycling the public water supply. But there isn't enough spring water for everyone. So what should we do? That's something you can explore in your story.

Other things in our water include chemical residues from plastic, radiation leaking from damaged nuclear plants and dumped nuclear waste, plastic microbeads, and all sorts of other pollutants. Where will it all lead? Can we clean it up before it's too late?

And what else might be in our water that we don't know about?

88. World-building

When you write science fiction and fantasy stories, you'll often need to invent a brand new world. A good starting point is to consider the underlying physics, chemistry, biology, geography, and geology of the planet.

You'll then need to design the landscape and settlements, and then think about different people, cultures, customs, laws, languages, and so on.

All of this is a heck of a lot of work. If you're only going to use this world in one story, you should consider making it an epic novel to get the most out of it.

But if it's a complex world and you've put a lot of time and effort into designing it, it makes more sense to use it for several stories. These can be epic novels, regular novels, novellas, short stories, screenplays, and so on. Turn them into a series, with each story set in the same world. It's a good idea to keep the same core set of characters too. Your readers will grow attached to them and they'll keep reading your work to find out what happens to them.

Another approach is to get together with other science fiction and fantasy writers and create a shared world. Each of you can then write stories set in that world. You might each have your own set of characters and write about different aspects of life there.

Sometimes you might write crossover stories, where the characters from one writer's series interact with those from another writer's series. This is a great way of introducing your readers to another writer's work, so they start reading those stories too. The other writers can of course return the favor and introduce their readers to your work.

If you don't know any science fiction or fantasy writers in the real world – or at least none that you'd like to build a shared world with – you'll find plenty of them online. Search for science fiction and fantasy writers' Facebook groups, and websites that have discussion forums. Look for writers that write the same sort of stories as you, then contact them to ask whether they'd be interested in designing a shared world.

It shouldn't take you long to assemble a small team. I'd suggest that your team should have between two and four members.

One other approach that's worth considering is to contact a writer that already has his own established world. If you enjoy the stories that take place in that world, and you think you'd like to set your own stories there, contact him and see if he'll allow it. Some writers will be happy to let you do this, while others will be fiercely protective of their worlds and won't let anyone else near them. But it's always worth asking the question.

And, as we saw earlier, there's always the possibility for collaborations and crossover stories where the two sets of characters interact.

Part 2: Storylines

89. Storyline: alien swarm

When astronauts land on a planet for the first time and find that the air is breathable, they remove their helmets and spacesuits. Shortly afterward they're attacked and bitten by swarms of tiny flies. This seems to be a minor irritation. But they have no idea that they're now part of the flies' breeding cycle.

When the flies bit them, they fed on their blood, just as mosquitos do on Earth, but they also deposited eggs under their skin. Humans are not a normal part of this species' breeding cycle, and things soon start to escalate.

The eggs hatch quickly, and the larvae grow at an enormous rate, with horrendous consequences. Perhaps the larvae begin eating the astronauts from the inside and release chemicals that affect their minds.

Now that their minds are no longer their own, they have no choice but to do what the larvae want. Perhaps they have to help the larvae move on to the next stage of their development, or find them a new host to live on.

What happens next is up to you.

How many of the astronauts die? Do any of them survive? If so, how?

Are they eaten completely, bones and all?

Perhaps the chemicals wear off once the larvae leave, and the astronauts' minds gradually return to normal. Will the parts of them that have been eaten grow back? Will next year's larvae "harvest" them all over again?

What if the chemicals permanently damaged their minds or affected them in some other way. For example, perhaps they're now infertile.

Perhaps the chemicals wiped the incident from the astronauts' memories. So when they're bitten by the flies again the following year – or whenever the flies' next breeding cycle is – they aren't expecting it and haven't taken any precautions. They also can't warn other astronauts who arrive on the planet.

What about the species that the flies usually lay their eggs in? Perhaps the larvae were killing them and keeping their numbers under control. But now that the flies are attacking humans instead, that other species might multiply at an alarming rate, causing all sorts of problems.

What else might happen?

90. Storyline: an hour a day

Our hero wakes up one day to find that his sense of time is out of sync with everyone else's.

For example, he might arrive at work by 9:00 a.m., complete an entire day's work, and find that it's not even 10:00 a.m. yet. Similarly, he might go to bed at 11:00 p.m., get a good night's sleep and wake up feeling refreshed and raring to go, only to find that less than an hour has passed and it's not yet midnight. What's going on?

If he does a whole day's work in under an hour, does that mean he can leave work early? Or does he have to stay there? Either way, he'll have plenty of spare time. Perhaps he could start his own business – or several of them – and make a fortune. After all, if he spends an hour a day on each of them, it's the equivalent of everyone else putting in a full day's work. Perhaps he could write a few novels while he's at it too. He could do all of these things while he's at work, and his employer might be none the wiser.

Or perhaps his employer knows exactly what's going on – and also know the reason why his life has suddenly sped up. His employer might even have caused it.

There are other questions we need to ask ourselves at this point:

- Has time simply sped up for him?

- If an entire day now lasts just three hours – for him at least – does he need to sleep for an hour every couple of hours?

- Is he aging eight times faster than everyone else?

- Has time sped up for anyone else? Or everyone else? If so, why haven't the clocks sped up too?

- If we sped up and the clocks sped up, would we even notice that time was moving faster?

- Did someone cause it? And if so, was it deliberate or an accident?

- If no one caused it, how did it happen?

- How do other people see him? Is he a fast-moving blur? Or does he move so quickly that they can't see him at all – as if he's a ghost?

When he looks at other people, do they seem to move really slowly? Or at normal speed? Perhaps he could use this to his advantage and break all sorts of speed records.

- Can he talk to anyone, or hear what they're saying? Or is his voice so fast and theirs so slow that they're unintelligible? Perhaps he can only communicate in writing.

He might find all of this fun at first – if somewhat confusing. He's many times more productive than everyone else. He's making a ton of money. And he has so much more time to get things done. He can take up all those hobbies he never thought he'd have time for. And, even better, he can afford to do them.

But there are drawbacks, of course. He might move so quickly that competing against other people is impossible: he always wins. Without the element of competition, taking part might seem pointless. Having a relationship with anyone will be difficult too – though not necessarily impossible.

Once the enjoyment has gone out of living like this, he might decide to search for an explanation and see if he can return to normal. But where will he even begin? And will he eventually succeed? Only you can decide.

91. Storyline: back to Earth?

Planet Earth was abandoned thousands of years ago. It was too polluted, its resources were drained, and it couldn't support the massive human population. So everyone was shipped to a new planet.

But now the planet they moved to is experiencing the same problems. In a few years, it will no longer be able to support the human population that currently lives there. It's time to move everyone to yet another planet.

Surprisingly, the Earth is one of the candidate planets they consider moving everyone to. No one has visited it for centuries, but according to their sensors it appears to have recovered completely.

Another option might be to split the population, with half of them returning to Earth and the remainder staying where they are.

However, although the Earth appears to have recovered, things are very different there now. What might have changed?

There might have been a cataclysmic event. Perhaps a super-volcano eruption, a massive rise in sea levels, a new ice age, a direct hit from an asteroid, or something else.

What if the nuclear power stations and weapons stores were abandoned rather than decommissioned when we left? They might have leaked or exploded and caused widespread contamination. Could humans even survive there now? We might need to send a crew on an exploratory mission to find out. Their leader could be the hero of your story.

Or perhaps the Earth has been colonized by aliens – and they're determined to keep intruders out.

Or perhaps something else has happened.

You can have a great deal of fun exploring all the possibilities. The best ones should lead to some terrific stories.

92. Storyline: clones

Someone has created some human clones and placed them all around the world. Why? Well, that's up to you. But none of them realize they're clones; they think they're regular people just like everyone else. But one day two of the clones find each other.

There are plenty of easy ways they could find each other. For example, they could upload their photos to a website or app that compares people's faces and matches them with others who look like them. These services already exist. Or they might have a shared interest – they are clones after all – and meet through that. Or someone might notice their resemblance and put them in touch with each other.

The clones are astonished to find each other, and they'll probably assume they're twins at first. They might question their parents about whether that could be the case. The people they call their parents aren't actually their parents at all, of course. Do their "parents" know their adopted children are clones? Do they know about the other clones?

DNA tests prove they're the same person, but that only leads to more questions. How many more of them there might there be? Who created them? Who were they cloned from? And why was he chosen as the "master copy" from which the others would be created?

When they discover that there could be more clones like them out there, the two clones set off on an amazing adventure. They want to track down the other clones – if they exist – and find the answers to their questions.

But when they find the answers, will they like what they hear? Probably not. So what will they do then? What will happen to them, and the other clones, in the end?

[NOTE] There's lots of scope for mistaken identity in this story. Whether you choose to make it a comedy is up to you, but the potential is certainly there.

93. Storyline: deadly fruit

A fruit farmer cross-breeds two species. The resulting fruit is delicious – but also deadly.

It seems harmless enough at first. But perhaps that particular combination of enzymes doesn't work well together. The enzymes in the new fruit slowly destroy your brain cells, wreck your nervous system, and ultimately kill you. Unfortunately, no one recognizes the danger until it's much too late.

You'll die from something that looks very much like bovine spongiform encephalopathy (BSE or "mad cow disease"). In fact, that's probably what doctors think it is at first. They'll probably blame the deaths on contaminated meat, and the initial investigation might focus on the beef supply chain.

As the new fruit is so delicious, it sells extremely well, and the fruit farmer makes a fortune. The fruit might even be slightly addictive. Scientists might recognize its addictive qualities but say it's a good thing because everyone should eat more fruit anyway.

When the fruit farmer dies, nothing untoward is suspected. He too seems to have been suffering from mad cow disease. But everyone knows you only get that from eating contaminated meat. No one even considers there might be a connection with the fruit. Sales continue to boom.

[NOTE] What if the fruit farmer is a vegan or vegetarian? He can't possibly have caught mad cow disease from eating contaminated meat. Why doesn't that trigger any alarm bells?

More and more people die. They all seem to have mad cow disease. And the situation rapidly becomes worse – a national or international disaster, with thousands, perhaps millions affected.

Scientists will eventually trace the problem to the fruit, but it might take them years. Perhaps the clue lies in the fact that everyone who dies from this new form of mad cow disease has an insatiable craving for the fruit. They might demand it even as they lie dying.

The connection is eventually made and proven, and the fruit is immediately withdrawn from sale. The whole crop is destroyed.

What will happen next, and how will the story end? Will everyone who has ever eaten the fruit die? Or do they need to have consumed a certain amount? Do some people have a built-in immunity to it?

Will a scientist – perhaps the hero of your story – create an antidote and save everyone? Or is it too late? Even if the antidote halts the disease in its tracks, people might have suffered permanent damage to their brains and central nervous systems. There might be a lot of severely disabled people around.

Does the disease only affect those with a particular pre-existing condition? That might even turn out to be a good thing, because if there's no one left alive who can pass it on to the next generation, the condition will be eradicated. Although it will, of course, be seen as a tragedy too.

[EXTENSION] If you want to add an extra layer of complication and villainy, how about if terrorists learn about the deadly enzymes? They might establish their own fruit farms, extract the enzymes from the fruit they harvest, and use them to create biological weapons.

94. Storyline: destination space

A spacecraft left Earth several hundred years ago and has been traveling through space ever since. Generations of people have been born, raised, lived, worked, reproduced, and died on board, but they still haven't reached their destination. Those that are on board now have no real concept of their planet of origin. All they have are photos, videos, and a few artifacts their ancestors brought with them. The only home they know is their spacecraft.

Where is the spacecraft going, and why? How was the original crew selected? When was it launched, and how much longer will it take to reach its destination? Will they arrive within the current crew's lifetime? Or do they just need to keep the ship pointed in the right direction, carry out routine maintenance, and reproduce so that one of their future generations will eventually reach their new home planet?

Occasionally, they might receive messages from Earth. Are these viewed with excitement, or with detachment? Presumably, there's less excitement with each passing generation, as they no longer have any emotional connection to their ancestors' home planet. Or perhaps there's great excitement – it's up to you.

How often do these messages arrive? Do they send a reply? If they do, perhaps one or two crew members might try to strike up a long-distance relationship with the people back on Earth. But how long does it take their messages to reach the Earth and for a reply to come back? It will of course take longer and longer as their craft travels further away.

What if the messages stop? Is it a temporary communications failure? Is the fault at their end or the Earth's end? Has something bad happened on Earth? Does it really matter? It's not as if they feel any great attachment to the place now. None of them will ever go back there. Though they might perhaps hope that their descendants might go back there one day.

What if the spacecraft goes through a radioactive dust cloud that renders everyone on board sterile? If they can't reproduce, their mission will have been in vain. There won't be any future generations to reach their new home planet. Can they do anything about it? Or is the mission now doomed?

Perhaps one or more parts of the craft are shielded against radiation. Which crew members were in those areas when the craft passed through the cloud? They might have been prisoners who were locked in a secure part of the ship. The entire mission might now depend on them.

Or perhaps the spacecraft is carrying frozen embryos in radiation-proof containers in case this sort of thing happened. The crew will now have to defrost them and put their backup plan into action.

[EXTENSION] As they've been in space for so long, they may have developed a few myths and legends. What are they, and do they have any real significance? Do they correlate with myths, legends or actual events on Earth? Or did someone on board invent them a few generations ago, and people have started to believe in them? How have they mutated from the original stories and events?

95. Storyline: DreamWorld

DreamWorld is a theme park set in virtual reality. You go along, pay your entrance fee, lie down and put on a headset, and enter a whole new world.

You can do anything you like in DreamWorld; there are no boundaries or limits. You can fly, you can breathe underwater, and you can ride impossible roller coasters. And, of course, you can have as much sex as you like with whoever you like. Or, if you prefer, you can kill people, carry out daring robberies, blow up buildings, and so on.

Unfortunately, the Dream World computer system has been hacked, and it's out of control. And it wasn't particularly reliable in the first place.

The owners know they should switch the system off and reset it. They should also upgrade the hardware, and install better security systems, safeguards, effective barriers between the "good" and "bad" areas of DreamWorld, and so on. But all of that would cost far too much money. Instead, they give users a panic button to wear on their wrists. Hit the button if things go wrong and you'll return to the start for a free replay. However, the buttons are no more reliable than the rest of the system, and they often don't work.

Users wanting good experiences and users wanting bad experiences sometimes come into contact with each other inside the virtual world. You could be happily making love when your luxury hotel gets blown apart at the worst possible moment. Or a gangster might take on the guise of your lover, so you end up making love to the wrong person – although she looks exactly the same.

Your story of DreamWorld can be an action-packed science fiction thriller with plenty of scope for comedy, romance, and even erotica.

You can focus on several groups of people:

- The customers who came along for a good experience but it turns bad.

- The customers who came along for a bad experience but it turns out much worse than they expected.

- The technical staff, both inside and outside DreamWorld, who strive to maintain order and keep the whole thing running – with limited success. Their level of success decreases as things spiral out of control.

- The owners, who won't let the technical staff shut down the system or spend the money to fix the problems. The staff have to manage with what they have. In fact, the owners would like them to find ways of saving even more money, and making more of it. It's all about the profits.

- The hackers who keep finding new ways of compromising the system.

Meanwhile, some people might be trapped inside DreamWorld. They might need to find and rescue their missing lovers. Their lovers might have been kidnapped by gangsters. They've tried hitting their reset buttons, but nothing happened.

Now they have no choice but to participate in the greatest adventure of their lives.

[NOTE] You might ask: why don't they just remove their headsets and return to the real world when things turn bad? The problem is that DreamWorld is such an immersive experience that it *is* the real world as far the users are concerned. The possibility that they could remove their headsets and leave never even occurs to them.

When their time inside the game runs out, everything turns black, a "game over" message appears, and they're shown a reorientation video to help them adjust to life back in the real world. At the end of the video, they're instructed to remove their headsets and wait for assistance.

Although they might "play" DreamWorld for only an hour or two at a time, it might feel as if days, weeks, months or even years are passing by once they're inside it.

96. Storyline: emergency landing

Your characters have landed on a planet unexpectedly. Perhaps their engine has failed and they have hardly any power or oxygen left. If the air on the planet is breathable, they might be able to carry out repairs and continue their journey. But if the air isn't breathable, they're doomed.

They might send out a probe to sample and analyze the planet's atmosphere. But just as it's preparing to transmit the data back to the spacecraft, its power fails too.

So now they have no idea whether the air outside is safe, and with night falling they have no way of finding out until tomorrow. They might have to spend the night inside their craft, with a dangerously low oxygen supply. They might not all survive. When the sun comes up tomorrow, it should recharge the probe's batteries, and it will be able to send them the data about the planet's atmosphere – assuming the spacecraft has enough power to receive it, which it might not. In the meantime, the information they need is stored in the probe's memory chips and is completely inaccessible.

Could they find another way of determining whether the air is breathable?

Could they rig up an alternative power source that would allow them to examine the probe's memory?

Could they send one of their more dispensable crew members outside to see if he survives? How do they determine who to send?

Could they find an alternative way of powering the spacecraft's life-support system so they can survive even if the planet's air isn't breathable?

Will they eventually solve at least some of these problems? If they find an answer, is it the one they were hoping for? Do they ever make it off the planet? Do they ever make it home? Presumably, some of them will – but maybe not all of them.

97. Storyline: glass performance artist

This is a strange one – I'll explain my thought process in a moment. It's the story of a performance artist in the future. He has his skin replaced with glass so that his organs and blood vessels are visible.

Is this a permanent thing, or is it just temporary? Is it reversible? If so, how will he get his skin back? What other problems might he encounter?

You might want to consider things like permanent nerve damage and loss of skin sensitivity, problems controlling his temperature, the glass getting fogged up by fat deposits, and so on.

Will he leave some skin on certain parts of his body, such as his hands, feet, head, and genitals? How much of his body will actually be on display?

How will his organs be visible beneath his skin? Won't his muscles and fat cells block the view? Or does he have those removed too? What problems might that cause him?

Will he remain in one place, perhaps under medical supervision, or will he go out in public? What will the public think? How can he get around if he's had his muscles removed? Does someone wheel him around on a trolley? Perhaps he just has a glass panel fitted in his chest and he can move around relatively easily.

If people have to pay to see him, will anyone come? How much money will he make? Will it be enough to cover his medical expenses? Will it make his fortune? Will he think it's worth it?

When his performance is over, and he has the glass removed and his skin replaced – and perhaps his muscles and fat cells too – how successful will that be?

Will he regret doing it? Will it damage him long-term – not just physically but mentally too? Or will he be perfectly fine and start planning an even more outrageous stunt for his next "performance"?

I'm not sure this would make a complete story, but it would make an interesting scene. And what a fantastic character! Perhaps the main characters in your story could go and see his performance. Or they might come across him in the street and stop to find out more. He might even provide them with a vital piece of information.

[GETTING IDEAS] You might be interested in how I came up with this idea. The hand basin in the men's toilet at our office was leaking, and someone had put a bucket under it to catch the drips until the plumber arrived. The bucket was dirty; it looked as if it had been used on a building site. I idly wondered what else it might have been used for and what sights it might have seen.

Then I thought of glass-bottomed buckets that allow you to see beneath the surface of water. And that led me to think of glass-bottomed boats. Which led me to the song *Fat-bottomed Girls* by Queen, but I changed the words to Glass-bottomed Girls. That led me to think of the song *Heart of Glass* by Blondie. And then the image of a glass-skinned performance artist popped into my head.

It pays to look around and let your mind wander sometimes.

98. Storyline: immediate answers

Our hero only has to ask a question or think about a mystery, and the answer is immediately given to him. Perhaps it's a voice inside his head, or perhaps it's telepathy, though he has no idea who could be giving him the answers, or why they might be doing it. This puzzles him – and troubles him too. But when he asks about it, there's no response. It's one of the few questions that doesn't get answered. Why is that? What other questions don't get answered?

Is someone watching him and feeding him the information? If so who, and why? How are they doing it?

Could the information be coming from the spirit world? Or a guardian angel?

Is it his own subconscious? If so, does that make him a genius?

Is it the voice of God? He's never been particularly religious, so he doesn't think so, but he can't rule it out entirely.

Could it be a strange form of madness? You might call it "madness with benefits."

Could he be picking up TV or radio broadcasts? Perhaps it's just a coincidence that they appear to answer his questions at exactly the right moment.

Could it be a computer that's been programmed to read and understand his thoughts and broadcast data back to him? If so, is it reading other people's thoughts too? How come no one else can hear what it broadcasts? Or maybe they can, but they never talk about it. Has our hero ever mentioned it to anyone? There might be thousands of other people like him. Does anyone else know this is happening to him?

Is there something special about him? Was he abducted in his sleep and a receiver implanted in his brain? Was he abducted by aliens? Is he the subject of someone's experiment? Is he a robot?

Or is he just hallucinating? Perhaps he's mentally ill or has a brain tumor.

Are the answers he receives always right?

You could take this story in any direction you like. He might be an alien or a robot or a cyborg or someone from a different time, or anything you like. Or he might just be an ordinary man who hears voices.

99. Storyline: in love with a man from the future

A man from the future time-travels back to the present day. He's a researcher and historian, and he wants to rebuild historical records from our time that have been lost.

He falls in love with a girl from the present day. Being from the future, he probably finds her somewhat earthy and unclean, and quite primitive in her ways – which rather excites him.

She tells him about her life, which he finds useful for his research. But she also tells him about the parts of her body she's unhappy with. He finds this fascinating too, because where he comes from everyone is perfect thanks to centuries of genetic modification.

He, in turn, tells her about his life, which she finds equally fascinating. After much persuasion, he agrees to take her home with him. But the only way to do this is to smuggle her through the time portal. Unfortunately, he gets caught and is thrown in jail when he arrives back in his time. The girl has to spend several months in quarantine. While she's there, she might be subjected to various tests so that the scientists of the future can learn more about the people from our time. And when she's eventually released from quarantine, she might be thrown in jail too.

In jail, she might be "decontaminated" to bring her up to the higher standard of cleanliness they have in the future. That might mean cleaning her mind as well as her body, purging her of impure thoughts. Her body might be thoroughly cleaned inside and out; even her DNA might be given a good scrub.

One day she wakes up to find that her body has changed. All the imperfections she moaned about have been fixed. How does she feel about that – especially as she didn't give them permission to change anything?

Once she's released from jail, will she enjoy living in the future? Will she enjoy living with the man? There are probably some things he hasn't told her. What are they? How will she feel about that? What if she demands to be sent back to her own time? Will they allow her to go?

If they send her home, they might erase her memory of her time in the future. She might be sent back to the exact moment that she originally left, so it appears that no time has passed.

Will they allow her to keep the modifications they made to her body? If anyone sees her time-traveling into the future and instantly returning – but looking strikingly different – what will they think? It will seem as if her face and body just reconfigured themselves.

But it's important to remember that they didn't just change her appearance. They scrubbed her from top to bottom, inside and out. So she might think and act differently now. She might appear to have a completely different personality.

How could her appearance and personality have changed in an instant? Again, she can't explain it, and nor can anyone else. Will she like the result? Will everyone else?

[EXTENSION] Will the man travel back into the past again to come and look for her? Perhaps he might decide to stay here with her this time. How will he cope with that? Will she recognize him? Will he like her as much now that she's the same as the other girls from his own time?

These two characters are probably the only two genetically perfect people on the planet – in our time at least. So it makes sense if they stay together. But do they recognize that this is the case? Are our current standards of genetic testing advanced enough to prove it?

100. Storyline: Jovian gas-beings

The characters in this story live on a gas planet – such as Jupiter or Saturn. There's no land; they spend their entire lives in the air.

What sort of creatures are they? Are they wispy filaments composed entirely of gas? Or are they solid? If they're solid, how do they stay in the air all the time?

> [IDEA] They might have built-in magnets that work in conjunction with the planet's magnetic field. They might be able to control their level of magnetism and float up and down in the air at will.

What sort of civilizations and social hierarchies have they built? Where do they live? Do they live and work in anything that we might recognize as a building or structure? Do they even work at all?

How do they eat or get nutrients? Perhaps they gain their energy from radiation, or gravity, or magnetism, or solar energy.

How do they reproduce?

How intelligent are they? Do they have any self-awareness? Do they have individual personalities?

How do they entertain themselves, play, fight, and so on? How do they misbehave or let off steam? Or do they not do that? What sort of adventures do they have that wouldn't be possible on solid ground?

If they live on one of the gas giants, the pressure will be immense unless they stay high in the atmosphere. If they go too low, the pressure will crush them, and the planet will absorb them. That might be what happens when they die, or if they become too ill to remain in the air.

On the other hand, when they die, they might simply break apart and drift away on the breeze.

[EXTENSION] If you can come up with enough adventures for these creatures, there's scope to turn this into a whole series of stories. Perhaps you could base your stories on an existing series of family sagas.

[NOTE] There's a genuine scientific theory that gas-creatures might live in the Earth's atmosphere. Perhaps they can be found throughout space.

101. Storyline: love and hate on Planet X

A spacecraft sets off to colonize another planet. The crew are all couples in stable relationships – or at least they were when they set off. But it's a long journey, and after several years crammed together in a small spacecraft, things change. They grow to hate each other.

Everything they need to establish their new civilization has been sent to the planet in advance. All they have to do is move in and start procreating. But that isn't going to happen, it seems – even when they're ordered to get on with it by their commanding officer. If they've decided to disobey him, there's not much he can do about it. He was probably in a stable relationship himself when they set off, but he isn't any more. So what will happen?

As there's no way of bringing them home, perhaps a second spacecraft could be sent from Earth. The plan might be that the new crew members will mate with those that are already on the planet.

That won't go to plan either though. There are all sorts of things that might go wrong. For example, the original crew might have killed each other by the time the second crew arrives. Or they might kill the new crew members who pair up with their former partners. They might hate their former partners, but that doesn't mean they'll let other people sleep with them. You can probably come up with a long list of other things that might go wrong. Pick the most interesting ones and build your story around them.

102. Storyline: meeting the dead

A scientist discovers that we don't actually die, we just slip into another dimension. He then finds a way of opening a portal into that dimension. He knows he's succeeded when he looks through the portal and sees his late brother peering back at him. Even better, they're able to talk to each other.

He charges people a hefty fee to use his portal to chat with their dead relatives. TV companies also use his portal to interview dead celebrities. What information and answers will the dead celebrities provide? Law enforcement agencies will be queuing up to use it too, so they can interview homicide victims and others who died unexpectedly.

As the waiting list of people wanting to use his portal grows longer and longer, the scientist realizes that he can make much more money by selling the devices which generate the portals. Those who are wealthy enough can then open portals in their own towns or cities, charge people to use them – thus becoming even richer – while providing people with a valuable service that's much in demand. The scientist soon becomes a billionaire several times over.

But there's trouble brewing on both sides of the portal. On the living side, spiritualists and mediums suddenly find themselves out of work, and they aren't happy about it. The people in charge of the dead side aren't happy either, as anyone can now contact the living. They tolerated it when a few spiritualists and mediums did it, but now everyone's doing it, and it's just not right. They decide to put a stop to it.

Let's say that the leaders of the dead and the spiritualists and mediums team up and arrange to destroy the devices. And let's say they manage to do that, but something goes wrong: the spiritualists and mediums can no longer contact the dead, and vice versa. Both sides are cut off from each other.

What might happen next? The living will be desperate to get back in touch with the dead, so they might rebuild the portals. Will the dead immediately destroy them again? Perhaps the spiritualists and mediums will go back into business, but they're all fakes now because they can't actually contact the dead any more.

There's another issue too, of course. Now that the living people know the dead are definitely there, and that death isn't the end, there will almost certainly be a massive increase in the number of suicides. Vast numbers of people will want to cross the divide and rejoin their loved ones. Can anything be done about that?

103. Storyline: memory swap

In a bizarre accident, a man has all of his memories replaced with someone else's. He can remember everything about his life with absolute clarity – except it isn't his life.

His personality survived the accident intact. So when he needs to make decisions and judgments, he uses his own personality but combines it with the other person's memories. The decisions and judgments he makes will obviously be different from the ones he would have made before the accident.

He can see nothing wrong with this: it all makes perfect sense to him. But those who knew him before the accident can tell that something is badly wrong. His personality is definitely his own, and his memories of general events and current affairs are all present and correct. But his memories of specific personal details are gone. They've been replaced with memories that bear no relation to his life. They make no sense at all. They probably sound like lies. His family might refer him to a psychiatrist.

So, who is this unfortunate man? How did the accident happen? How did he end up with someone else's memories? Does someone else now have his memories?

Perhaps he was taking part in an experiment that went wrong. Does he know what has happened to him? Does he realize anything is wrong? Does he notice that the people around him act strangely when he talks to them? Does he even know who they are?

Perhaps he moves away and starts living the other person's life. If he's swapped memories with someone else, that other person might start living his life. Will that be a permanent arrangement? Are they happy about it? Is everyone else happy about it?

Is there a cure? Can the memory swap be reversed? What if the other person won't agree to the reversal because he likes our character's memories better than his own? Will our character keep the other person's memories? Or will he ask to have his memory erased so he can start again from scratch? At least he'll know his memories are all his own if that happens.

Does the technology to erase someone's memories exist in your story world? And will it work without harming him?

What if one person keeps the other person's memories, but the other person has his own memories restored? Now they'll both have exactly the same memories.

104. Storyline: nerve cells

In a world with no metal, how do the inhabitants send information around the planet?

They might have started off with smoke signals and semaphore, but they've progressed beyond that. They send their information electronically now. The problem is that the only things capable of carrying electrical signals might be nerves taken from animals.

Human nerves might be especially prized because of their length and the fact that they work at such high speeds. Communications workers on that planet might abduct people from Earth, breed them on farms, and then harvest them for their nerves.

Perhaps nerves from other creatures – such as worms or snakes – could be used for the majority of the network. Human nerves might only be used when higher speeds are required.

But customers might be calling for increased speeds across the entire network. The only solution is to rebuild the entire network with human nerves. And that's going to mean mass abductions and a massive breeding and harvesting program.

One other question you'll need to answer is how they get the information into the nerves and how they decode it when it reaches the other end. No metal means no electronics. So how do they do it?

Well, if they're abducting humans from Earth, they could collect some metal while they're there. They won't be able to carry enough of it to make cables for their network, but it might be enough to build the electronic components they need.

But that leads to the next question: when they travel to Earth for the first time, what do they build their spacecraft from? If there's no metal on the planet, how can they do this? And how can they build the guidance, launch and propulsion systems?

They're an ingenious species: they'll figure something out.

> **[NOTE]** If you can't figure out a way of doing this, just have a space probe from Earth land on their planet. They can adapt that.

One other option for sending the information is to not use electronics at all. You could have two people's brains connected together by really long strands of nerves. You give the person at your end the message you want to send, he reads it and transmits it – by thinking about it – to the person at the other end of the strand of nerves. The person at the other end then either speaks the message or writes it down.

105. Storyline: new metal

A new type of metal arrives on Earth. Perhaps it arrives on a meteorite or a crashed spaceship. The metal is beautiful and extremely valuable. Once scientists have taken all the samples they need for analysis, there's still some left over. So they decide to sell it to the public. It will be ideal for making jewelry, and the sale will raise a significant amount of money to fund other research projects.

Let's say that the metal has to be heated to several thousand degrees before it can be manipulated. This is a much higher temperature than a jewelry maker could achieve, so the scientists make the jewelry themselves in their laboratory. They might recruit a master jeweler to advise them.

But they run into an unforeseen problem: once the metal has been heated to that degree, it shrinks if it's exposed to sunlight for prolonged periods. In fact, it shrinks suddenly, rapidly, and with considerable force. If you happen to be wearing a ring made from this metal, you're going to lose your finger.

Unfortunately, quite a few people *do* wear rings made from the metal. And, sure enough, the rings shrink when they've been exposed to the sun for a while. Several people lose their fingers.

Naturally enough, they want compensation. The rings themselves cost an absolute fortune, and they've shrunk to a fraction of their former size, so they're worth considerably less now. And, of course, they want compensation for the loss of their fingers too.

The scientists manage to recover most of the metal – much of it from hospitals after people have had their fingers amputated.

The rapid contraction issue might actually turn out to be useful in certain industrial applications. So they might manage to sell the metal again – though for much less money this time. They might make just enough to settle the compensation claims, but they'll end up with nothing themselves. None of the research projects they were planning will now get funded.

And of course, they still have the guilt of causing all of those unfortunate people to lose their fingers. Most of the victims were the wives and mistresses of wealthy and highly influential figures. The negative publicity could set science back by many years.

106. Storyline: new moon

When a new moon eases into orbit around the Earth, there's enormous excitement. Initially, there was wide-spread panic that it was going to crash into the Earth and wipe out all of civilization. But astronomers soon realized it was traveling far too slowly to pose much of a threat. They kept revising their calculations as it drew nearer, and eventually confirmed that it would be captured by the Earth's gravity, enter permanent orbit, and become a moon.

Although not terribly large, the moon's mass turns out to be much higher than expected. It's densely packed with valuable metals and minerals. But its strong gravitational field wreaks havoc on Earth, causing massive tides, flooding, and earthquakes. Its strong magnetic field is disastrous too, disrupting unshielded communications, upsetting compass-based direction-finding systems, sending migratory birds thousands of miles off-course, and causing undesirable atmospheric effects.

The best solution, some scientists suggest, would be to break the new moon up and bring the pieces down to Earth. Not only would most of the problems cease, but we'd be able to access the vast riches within it.

It's going to be a slow process though, and hugely expensive – although whoever wins the contract will make their investment back many times over by selling the metals and minerals.

But the question then arises as to who owns this new moon, and who should have the right to profit from it. Some say it belongs to everyone, and everyone on Earth should therefore be given a share of the profits. But, of course, politicians and the owners of mining companies disagree. They want all of the profits for themselves.

With multiple countries vying for the rights to own, mine and exploit the new moon, it's the sort of thing that could lead to a world war.

And then there's the issue that the sudden flood of precious metals and minerals onto the world's markets might devalue or destabilize them. That could cause the world's economies to collapse. So, instead of everyone becoming richer, everyone might be plunged into poverty.

But there may be a simple solution. The chunks of moon are incredibly dense. If they're brought down to Earth, they'll have to be distributed evenly around the world. If they were all put in one place, they could throw the Earth off balance, change the speed of the planet's rotation, have untold effects on the magnetic field and gravity, and who knows what else. The only safe option is to give everyone a fair share.

In the meantime, while all of this is being debated and argued over, and even after the mining begins, the new moon is having potentially disastrous effects upon the Earth.

There are lots of issues for you to address here, and it should make a really exciting and intriguing story.

[EXTENSION] You might like to consider where this new moon came from. How and why has it ended up in orbit around the Earth? Is it on its own or are there any more of them out there? And if so, are any of them headed our way? Are they traveling at a safe speed? Are some of them coming too fast to go into orbit, meaning that they're likely to hit us? Is someone – or something – deliberately sending them in our direction? Do they have good intentions? Or sinister ones?

107. Storyline: rebuilding life

A scientist with strong religious convictions believes it's a sin to harm any of God's creatures. But one day he accidentally steps on a beetle and crushes it. From that moment on, he devotes himself to rebuilding the insect and bringing it back to life.

How does he fund this? Does he do it in his spare time? Does he manage to secure a grant? Does he have savings or an inheritance or another source of income that will cover his expenses while he does this?

Using a powerful microscope and tiny tools – some of which he has to invent – he painstakingly pieces the insect back together. At first, he might have to work in near-freezing conditions to prevent the insect from decomposing. Later he might buy or invent a device that keeps the insect cool while he works on it in a warm room.

Slowly and painstakingly, he repairs its crushed internal organs, reconnects its blood vessels and nerves, rewires its brain, replaces all its lost fluids, rebuilds its exoskeleton, and repairs its broken wings. Finally, after many years, he finishes the job. Remarkably, the insect comes back to life.

When he announces what he has done, he wins all sorts of awards and is celebrated in the media. But what happens next?

People will obviously want him to bring their dead relatives back to life. He can't do that – yet – but surgeons should be able to use some of the techniques he has developed to save more people's lives.

People will also want him to bring their dead pets back to life. Again, he can't do that yet. But he needs a new challenge, so he might select just one of them and give it a try.

Or perhaps he might try upgrading the insect he saved. Could he make it better than it was before? What parts will he upgrade?

Or perhaps he'll try creating a brand new insect from scratch. If he can do such a thing, not only will he believe in God, he might actually *be* a god himself – at least according to some people. What will he think about that? What will other people think – especially the religious ones?

108. Storyline: space crew

The main character in this story must select a crew for a long space journey. He'll need a captain, pilots, navigators, communications specialists, engineers, scientists, and so on. It's a big spacecraft with a large crew, so he'll also need to select maintenance and housekeeping staff, medics, caterers, hairdressers, and so on. If you decide to make the spacecraft really big, he'll also need one or more human resources managers, admin staff, and more. If there are shops on board, he'll need people to run those too.

How will he select his officers? Will they come from the main pool of astronauts, or will he recruit them externally? Should external companies be invited to tender for the various contracts? If that happens, how can he be sure that the winning contractors have vetted their staff as rigorously as they were instructed to? Should he vet the staff again himself, just to make doubly sure?

What if a rogue employee slips through the net? He might need to employ some security officers too. Does the spacecraft have a prison cell? If not, should he put in a request to have one added?

To keep the number of staff to a minimum, he might select people who are multi-skilled. So he will look for engineers who are also qualified medics, navigators who can also operate the communications systems, admin staff who can also cut hair, and so on.

As the journey will take several years, he'll need to make sure each crew member is absolutely sure they want to sign up. They'll be away from their family and friends for an awfully long time.

You could have two plot lines running throughout the story:

The main plot will be all about selecting the right crew. Depending on the length of the story, and whether you plan to make it a series, that section might take up a few chapters, the first act, or the whole book.

Later chapters, acts or books might cover the outward journey and the various adventures they have on the way, the things they do when they reach their destination, the return journey – if there is one, and the homecoming. Some crew members will get on well with the others, but others might not interact so well. There will undoubtedly be disputes, and probably a few fights too. Perhaps there will be some murders and other crimes – it's up to you. But who will investigate them?

The second plot-line might follow a few of the crew members more closely. You'll show them spotting the advertisement for a role on the spacecraft, applying to join it, being interviewed, tested and vetted, and getting selected. Then you could show them weighing up the pros and cons of going on the long journey, deciding what to take with them, saying goodbye to their friends and family, and so on. Then you'll follow them throughout the journey, focusing on them throughout the story, but also mentioning the other crew members too.

In the first section of the story, you could also follow some of the people who apply but don't get selected.

109. Storyline: statues

The world is slowly – very slowly – being taken over by a race of strange beings. They might or might not be alien in origin. Everyone is well aware of them, but they're not the least bit worried because they know them as The Statues.

The Statues move, but not on the same time-scale as the rest of us. In a single human lifetime, a Statue won't appear to move at all.

They reproduce by getting humans with the right artistic skills to become sculptors. The sculptors carve new Statues from raw rock, though they never fully understand what they're doing. The Statues secretly guide them to cut the right shapes.

The Statues are waiting; biding their time. They'll still be here long after the humans who gave them life have died.

The only thing that bothers the Statues is the weather, which gradually erodes and disfigures them. And pigeons of course.

What will the Statues get up to in your story? Will they slowly but surely take over the world? Will they use their secret mind control techniques on anyone other than sculptors? Perhaps they've been doing exactly that for thousands of years, controlling us and directing the course of history.

Do they have a special bond with the sculptors who created them? How does that work? What happens when the sculptor dies? Is the bond broken? Does the Statue gain its freedom or extra powers? Can it move slightly faster? Can it alter its appearance slightly? If the sculptor made a mistake, can the Statue correct it once the sculptor has died?

110. Storyline: suicide 1 – time travel

In this story, a character decides to commit suicide by traveling back in time and getting his mother to fall in love with someone other than his father. The result will be that he was never born. He assumes he will simply disappear.

He completes his mission, but he doesn't disappear. Perhaps he needs to return to the present day, he thinks. He does so, but he finds that everything is exactly the way he left it, and he's still very much alive.

There's only one conclusion: the man he made his mother fall in love with must have been his real father. So who is the man he knows as "Dad"?

Perhaps his mother had an affair with his real father. But was that before or after she married the man he calls Dad? He might need to make several more trips into the past to find out the truth. And the truth might turn out to be startling and unexpected.

In fact, their relationships might be so confused and tangled that it takes him the entire story to work it all out. The fact that he time-travels into the past might be a vital element: he could be the key figure that leads to his own birth.

And now that he knows who his real father is, he might no longer feel the need to kill himself.

[NOTE] Don't make him his own father. That's been done plenty of times already.

But he could be someone else's father. What if he discovers he's his girlfriend's father? That would really complicate things.

Or how about if he was cloned from his father? Is his father technically his father in that case? Of course, that still doesn't explain who the man called "Dad" is. Was he the scientist that cloned him? Was he adopted? Does this mean he isn't related to his mother at all?

You might be able to come up with some better ideas.

111. Storyline: suicide 2 – depressed clone

This story is about a man who's a clone, but he doesn't know it. He might believe his father is dead. Perhaps he never knew who his father was. He might be one of the first human clones or maybe even the very first one. Because of this, his health and movements have been monitored ever since he was born. The monitoring might have been done with his full knowledge and cooperation, or it might have been done secretly.

But now he wants to commit suicide. The scientists monitoring him – one of whom might be the man he was cloned from – will, of course, be alarmed by this. How do they discover he wants to commit suicide? Does he tell anyone? Does he buy something that makes them think he intends killing himself?

The scientists might believe he's suffering from some sort of mental aberration caused by the cloning process. They have him admitted to a psychiatric hospital so they can find out. He'll have therapy to try to find out the reason for his suicidal thoughts, and – hopefully – find a cure. Most importantly though, he'll be closely monitored and won't be able to commit suicide while he's there.

But then the man they cloned him from reveals that it wasn't an aberration from the cloning process after all. He felt suicidal when he was that age too. He's never admitted it before, and it takes considerable courage for him to reveal it. It might even jeopardize his career.

But why did he feel suicidal? The reason might be bizarre or disturbing.

Perhaps he could somehow sense that one day his clone would have suicidal thoughts. And that knowledge triggered his own suicidal thoughts in a strange backward-flowing feedback loop.

Is this the first time such a thing has happened? Will the scientists be able to study it? Will their findings reveal anything else about the world?

112. Storyline: teleporting and cloning

A scientist has developed a way of teleporting people from one place to another. However, he doesn't actually move people as such; he scans them in and then creates a copy in another location using a type of 3D printer. Once the copy has been verified as complete and accurate, he destroys the original. This will obviously lead to all sorts of objections and legal wrangling. Is he committing homicide?

The system he invents can perform a high-speed, three-dimensional, full-body atomic/molecular scan, and then recreate it at the other end of the line using a molecular 3D printer. How long does it take to print the copy?

One of the biggest problems he had to solve was how to stop the parts that had already been printed from collapsing and leaking all over the floor while the rest of the body was still being printed. He might have developed some sort of freeze-ray to hold them in place. Or perhaps they're held in a magnetic field.

His process might eventually be approved. Or if not, he might just go ahead with it anyway.

But he might then refine it so that the person who gets printed at the other end isn't an exact copy. For example, the original person might have cancer tumors, but the copy doesn't. He might – in theory at least – be able to cure any disease by "teleporting" the person from one place to another. He might also be able to heal wounds and mend broken bones, replace missing limbs, cure paralysis, and even remove tattoos. All he as to do is alter the data in the computer file during the transfer process. It's all highly laudable and worthy of several Nobel Prizes ... except that the original person who gets scanned into the system gets killed. And that's the big crunch factor. Many people won't accept it – and certainly not the Nobel Prize committee. It's a step too far.

But if the original person isn't destroyed then he hasn't created a teleportation device, he's created a device for making clones. That might be just as good – or perhaps even better.

[ALTERNATIVE 1] His teleportation experiment has just worked successfully for the first time. He decides not to destroy the original person for 24 hours while he carries out some additional verification. Or perhaps he delays it simply because he wants to celebrate, and he gets drunk. Or perhaps he has to get drunk to build up enough courage to kill the original person.

But what will the original person do during those 24 hours? Perhaps, now that he's had time to think about it, he's realized that he doesn't want to be destroyed. Did he know his original body would be killed when he agreed to take part in the experiment? Did the scientist make it clear that this was part of the deal?

The original and the copy/clone are now two separate individuals. The original might try to contact the copy, either through conventional means or through telepathy. Will he track down the copy and persuade him to be the one that gets destroyed instead? Will he try to convince the scientist to kill the copy?

Or perhaps he'll make the most of being in two places at once for the next 24 hours. What sort of things will he and the copy get up to?

Let's say that the original still fears for his life. He might try to get the copy into trouble, perhaps causing someone to kill him. Or maybe he'll go on the run. Maybe they'll both go on the run. Let's explore that option. What if one of them gets arrested at some point in the future? Will the police know which version they've arrested? Will they even be aware that there are two of this person? Are there any differences between them?

What if one of them is convicted of homicide and is sentenced to death? Which one is it? If it's the original, then he was supposed to die anyway. If it's the copy, then the original will survive, so he'll have achieved his aim. Did he have anything to do with the homicide and the copy's arrest and conviction?

Or how about if the police capture both the original and the copy? Once the case has been processed by the courts – and that will be an intriguing case to write about – the verdict might be that only one of them can live. Who gets to decide? The judge? The jury? The scientist? The original person?

Let's say it's the scientist. Will he let the original live and agree to destroy the clone? And even if he agrees, will he actually go through with it? If the court orders him to destroy the copy, will he actually kill the original anyway – just as he'd planned to all along? And will anyone but the copy realize what he's done? Will the copy even know the original has been destroyed if he isn't there to witness it?

If the original person and the copy never meet, will the copy know he's a copy? Or will he assume he's the original person who went through the teleportation machine? He might have no idea that the original person still exists. After all, the teleportation machines he's read about in science fictions stories didn't work like that; they always disassembled the person, teleported his atoms and molecules to the new location, and then reassembled him. There were never two separate people, and no one ever got killed – unless the machine went wrong.

[NOTE] If no one can tell the difference between the original and the copy, the scientist might alter his device so that they're always distinguishable from now on. Just in case this issue happens again.

[ALTERNATIVE 2] The teleportation has taken place successfully. The copy has materialized at his destination, and the original person has been destroyed ... except he hasn't. The destruction mechanism has failed, but no one has realized it.

The original person is still alive, though unconscious. He wakes up after the laboratory staff have left for the evening, and he's able to walk free. He doesn't know he's been copied; he thinks the teleportation failed.

But his identity has been transferred to the copy, so he no longer officially exists. He and the copy might share a single identity – perhaps without either of them realizing it.

Identity theft happens in our world, so it might be just like that, except that the person he's stealing the identity from is himself. Who would ever know? Well, the original person probably will when he discovers that his personal records and bank balance aren't what they're supposed to be. What will he do about it?

113. Storyline: the book of life

Imagine that you found a book that records all the events in your life – including the parts that are still to come. Naturally, you'll turn straight to the end, where it says you'll live a happy, healthy life and die in your sleep at the age of 104. Well, that means it must be perfectly safe for you to jump in front of this bus that's coming down the street right now. So you try it. And you're completely unharmed, just as the book said you would be. But what happened to the bus and all the people on board?

How did you come across this mysterious book? Were you meant to see it?

Perhaps you were seriously injured and were having a near-death experience. You saw Heaven, and you liked it so much that you wanted to stay. But the people in charge of Heaven said you had to go back and live your life on Earth for a few more years. Perhaps you refused, and you got into an argument with them. But then you wondered how they knew when you were meant to die. And in the heat of the moment, they accidentally revealed that they had this book. You insisted on seeing it. Perhaps you would only agree to return to your mangled body – and possibly endure years of painful surgery to repair it – on condition that they let you see the book.

They eventually agreed. And you returned to your body. And perhaps you made an immediate and miraculous recovery and didn't need any surgery after all.

Now that you know you're pretty much indestructible until the age of 104, what will you do?

114. Storyline: the camera never lies

A scientist is trying to design a new type of camera, but he isn't having much success. His latest version doesn't even capture images properly; it's showing things that aren't really there. Not realizing the implications, he throws it away and goes back to the drawing board. But when he thinks about it later, he realizes what those implications might be.

He rushes back to his lab in the middle of the night, hugely excited, retrieves the camera from the trash, and studies the images again. His mind is racing. Could it be doing what he thinks it's doing?

Over the next few days, he uses the camera to take photos of people who have lost limbs in accidents. The photos show them with their limbs intact. He repeats the test with people who were born without those limbs. This time the camera doesn't add the missing limbs. What's going on? Could it be capturing their genetic code and displaying the result? Could it be capturing the person's thoughts about how their body should look? Or is something else going on?

He photographs a woman whose face was badly disfigured in a fire. The resulting photos show her as the beautiful woman she was before the fire. He falls in love with the image and, as a result, falls in love with the woman herself. He would never have fallen in love with her if he hadn't seen the photo.

But is it a true image of what she used to look like? Or is it an image of what she thinks she should look? Or is it what her DNA says she should look like? Or is it something else?

[NOTE] It's worth noting that while her DNA might dictate her general appearance, environmental factors and other circumstances in her life will also have played a significant part. For example, if she's had a hard and difficult life, and endured hardship and loss, she'll look much older than she would if she'd had an easier, happier time.

Let's say that she shows him a regular photo of herself before the fire, and she looks nothing like the image his camera produced. Perhaps she was rather plain and ordinary in real life, and not the slightest bit beautiful. So what the heck has his camera produced? And will he still love her?

[ALTERNATIVE] You can of course skip that last bit if you prefer. Perhaps in your story, she was beautiful in real life too.

115. Storyline: thought dictator

A ruthless dictator insists on knowing and controlling the thoughts of all his loyal – and not so loyal – subjects. But what sort of life would he have? And what sort of life would his citizens have? Will he continuously monitor every little thought? That would occupy all his time; he'd have to be truly obsessed. And, of course, he'd have no time to do anything else.

Perhaps he's brainwashed everyone so they can't think any disloyal thoughts. All he has to do now is listen out for the occasional rogue thought and give that person some extra brainwashing.

Does he brainwash everyone, or does he leave some of his most trusted friends and advisers alone? That might depend on how paranoid he is. If he leaves his friends and advisers alone, what's to stop them from seizing power one day? Could they brainwash him? Can they know his thoughts?

But if he brainwashes absolutely everyone, what sort of place would it be? Who could he talk to? No one would ever disagree with him. He wouldn't be able to have arguments or debates. Life would soon get boring, wouldn't it? It might seem a good idea at first, but the reality might not be the utopia he expected. Can he do anything to fix it? Or is it too late? Or is he perfectly happy with the way things are?

116. Storyline: time travel 1 – stranded in the Stone Age

A group of time travelers has been stranded in the Stone Age by a villain who has returned to his own time and taken the only time-travel device with him. Somehow, they need to return to the present. They realize that between them they have the knowledge and the ability to make the parts to build a time machine. It's going to take them a while though, and the device will be enormous, and incredibly crude, as they won't be able to create any micro-electronics. But it should just about work.

They'll need to locate various metal ores, build a furnace to smelt it, make molds to cast it, and so on. What about power? Well, there's plenty of fruit around, and as any science student knows, you can create electricity by sticking electrodes into fruit. If you need a lot of electricity, all you need is a lot of fruit. Or at least that's what they hope.

Of course, they only need to send one person back to the present. He can then return with a modern time-traveling device and collect the rest of them.

Or perhaps they only need to send a written message back to their own time, in the hope that someone will read it and come to their rescue. That might be the safest option. They might try that a few times. But when no one comes, they realize that they're going to have to send someone. Why did no one come? Didn't the message get through? Did they send it to the wrong time or place? Is their machine incorrectly calibrated? Did the villain intercept it?

So, will they manage to build the machine and return to their own time? Or will it send them to a different time? Or will it blow up and kill them all? Or will it fail to work at all, and leave them permanently stranded?

Perhaps they end up arguing and killing each other, and the machine is never completed.

Perhaps someone or something else kills them. Perhaps they're abducted by aliens. Perhaps someone from their time finds out what the villain did and comes back to rescue them. Or perhaps the villain himself comes back to save them five years later. But it might be too late by then.

117. Storyline: time travel 2 – no regrets

Do you have any regrets? The main character in this story does. He's reached a particularly unhappy point in his life, and he looks back on all his past mistakes and missed opportunities. Fortunately, he has access to a time machine so he can go back and put things right.

He has a few options. Which one will he choose? He could go back and relive the experience but do things differently this time around. Or he could send himself a note containing advice. Or he could meet up with his old self and have a chat about making the right decisions and taking advantage of certain situations. Perhaps he tries each of these, depending on the particular regret he's trying to fix.

What regrets does he have, and which of them will he attempt to fix first? What does he consider his biggest regret? Will he start with that one? Or will he go back to his earliest regret and work forward?

If he changes the outcome of an event, how will it affect the course of his life? Perhaps he won't need to fix every regret on his list because when he changed the outcome of the first event, the next one never happened.

Or perhaps, when he tries to change an outcome, something else happens instead. That option might not have been available to him the first time he experienced the event. And he might not know what he's supposed to do about it. Why does he have this extra option now? Why didn't he have it the first time?

He's bound to notice that changing the outcome of one event has an effect on all the others. So he'll probably decide to return to his own time after each change to see how things turned out. Or at least that would be the sensible option. He can then decide whether he needs to go back and change the next event on his list.

How will his life have changed each time he returns to the present? Is it a significant change, or a minor one? If he doesn't like the change, will he go back to the same event and try to affect the outcome again? And what if he still doesn't like it? He might have to spend years fixing a single event before he's happy with the result. But perhaps he only needs to change that one event and all his other regrets will be taken care of. Or perhaps it creates many other regrets and he never fixes them all. Some of his new regrets might be worse than his original ones.

What if the time machine isn't his and he's been accessing it illegally? If someone finds it switched on, they might switch if off while he's in the past. Does that mean he'll be stranded there?

And what if Mother Nature or fate fights back? Perhaps, despite all the changes he makes, his life still turns out exactly the same in the end. It just happens in a slightly different way.

118. Storyline: time travel 3 – quantum theory

It's a well-known fact that if you travel faster than the speed of light you effectively go back in time. But the distances and speeds involved are incredible. If you could travel from the Earth to the Sun in the blink of an eye, you'd effectively go back in time by around eight minutes. Let's say that you can somehow do this.

And let's say that you reach the Sun, trigger some kind of signal – a solar flare, for example – and immediately return to Earth. You were only gone for an instant, and when the solar flare is seen several minutes later, you can pretend you had nothing to do with it. Why you'd want to do this is something you'll need to explain in your story.

Since traveling that distance in such a short time is currently impossible, you'll need to find another way of doing it. Perhaps something from quantum theory might help.

According to the theory, if an object is quantum-linked, doing something to one half of it causes the other half to react in exactly the same way at exactly the same moment. The other half could be millions of miles away, and it will still work. So you could achieve the effect of time travel as long as the two halves of the quantum-linked object were far enough apart. And you wouldn't need to go anywhere.

Let's continue our earlier example. You could quantum-link something that triggered a solar flare, then send half of it to the Sun and keep the other half here on Earth. When you trigger the half that remained on Earth, you'd instantly trigger the solar flare on the Sun. We wouldn't see the effect here on Earth for over eight minutes. Of course, you'd have to hope – and ensure – that triggering it here wouldn't destroy the Earth.

Try playing around with this idea. You might come up with something amazing.

119. Storyline: voice command confusion

In this – possibly comic – vision of the future, every household appliance can speak, and they all respond to voice commands. That could lead to all sorts of chaos around the house when they start recognizing and responding to commands issued by other appliances.

Perhaps everything is fine until one particular appliance is added to the collection. The new appliance upsets the balance, and now all the machines chatter away to each other, respond to each other's commands, issue warnings, switch on an off at random, and switch things on and off around the house.

Perhaps the new appliance fits in perfectly well for the first few weeks, but then someone asks it to do something. They might use a phrase that hasn't been spoken in the house before. And it might trigger a tsunami of responses that sets off the other appliances and makes the place completely uninhabitable. And that's when everything is working correctly. What the heck might happen if they go wrong?

120. Storyline: weather beaters

Scientists have found a way of protecting the entire country from severe weather. How do you think it might work? One option might be to erect a coast-to-coast network of antennae that blast powerful electrical currents or radio frequency waves into the air. They'll break up storm clouds or prevent them from forming if the storm conditions look likely.

But what if the storm doesn't disperse? What if the system doesn't work? Have billions of dollars been wasted? Who will get the blame, and what will the consequences be? Why did it work during laboratory tests and field trials but not at full scale? What if the system makes storms more powerful?

What if the storm moves somewhere else rather than being broken up? If another country starts getting all of our storms, they aren't going to be happy about it. They might even erect a system of their own. Where will the storms go then? Will they be passed on to the next country down the line? Or will they bounce back and forth between the two countries?

Running the system will require a vast amount of electricity. Where will it come from? And won't people object to the antennae? They're such eyesores, and they're so big that they're visible from miles away. One solution might be to erect them only when a storm threatens. They might retract into the ground the rest of the time. It'll add billions to the cost, but it might be the only way of getting permission to erect them.

What effect might the powerful bursts of electricity or radio waves have on things like satellites, TV and radio, mobile and cellular communications, people, wildlife, hospital equipment, emergency services, aircraft, radar, military systems, and so on?

Perhaps the scientists who invent the system are never allowed to use it. But they might try it anyway, perhaps in another country where storms are more severe. They might set up a full-size test system in a remote area where it won't upset anyone. Will they ask for permission or will they just go ahead anyway? After all, it's often easier to apologize afterward than to get permission first. The country might even welcome them. But what if the system causes billions of dollars' worth of damage?

What else might go wrong? For a more interesting and exciting story, have the system fail in the biggest and most spectacular way possible.

And what if a spy satellite spots the sudden massive burst of energy and assumes it's a nuclear attack or something similar? The satellite operators and the military haven't been warned about the test. As far as they're concerned, this is a genuine threat. What will happen next?

[EXTENSION] If the system can be made to work, and the scientists can get permission to install it, they might make further refinements. For example, it might become possible to direct rain clouds to areas that need them and away from areas that don't. That might be done by altering the pattern of the electrical currents between antennae, creating waves that mimic weather fronts and air currents. But, again, consider what might go wrong.

121. Storyline: why aliens think the Earth is dead

Aliens from a far-distant planet arrive on Earth and survey it for signs of life. These aliens aren't carbon-based creatures like ourselves though. Let's say they're based on sulfur – you can obviously choose a different element if you want to. Although they detect small amounts of sulfur on Earth, there isn't enough to sustain life. There's almost none in the atmosphere and no evidence that sulfur-based life-forms ever evolved or existed here. They conclude that the Earth is barren and dead.

But why can't they see the carbon-based life-forms? What do they make of the buildings, cities, vehicles, trees, and grass? Why don't they recognize them as signs of civilization and life? Perhaps these things just look like rocks or sand to them.

Perhaps they don't send any aliens, just an autonomous rover. It might be similar to the ones we've sent to Mars. Again, it's only been programmed to search for sulfur-based life-forms. It will ignore everything else. Since there aren't any sulfur-based organisms on Earth, it will conclude that the planet is dead. It might return to its spacecraft and move on to the next planet. It might have better luck on Venus – there's lots of sulfur there. Even if it doesn't find any life, at least it will have plenty of interesting things to look at.

Now, as it stands, this isn't much of a story so far. It's probably more of a subplot or an interesting scene than a full story. So we need to do some more work on it to see if we can develop it further.

If you were writing the story, what would happen next? Here's my suggestion – which you're welcome to use or adapt.

Perhaps some of our scientists come across the rover and try to work out where it's from and what it's doing here. They might assume it's from another country at first, and that it's some sort of device for espionage. Will they take it apart and study it? Since it isn't carbon-based, does the material it's made from cause them any harm? What about the components inside? Does it have any self-defense mechanisms?

When they've finished studying it, will they put it back together again and release it? Will it lead them to the alien spacecraft? What will they do when they find it? Can they capture it and study it? Or will it take off before they have the chance?

What if some of the scientists are on board when it takes off? What will become of them? The spacecraft is presumably built from sulfur-based materials too. Will it harm the scientists? Is there any oxygen on board? Probably not if it's just a vehicle for ferrying the rover between planets. Will the scientists be able to survive for more than a few minutes?

It's starting to turn into much more of a story now. Have a play around with it and see where it takes you.

122. Storyline: you be me

Two people are about to get married, but before they take the plunge, they want to ensure their prospective spouses are everything they seem to be. Fortunately, a newly developed system can allow someone else's soul into your body, so they can experience what it's like to be you. And, of course, your soul can also enter their body, and you can see what it's like to be them. You'll also find out all their dirty little secrets – and they'll find out yours. What will they find out? Have they been completely honest with each other?

The man's soul can leave his partner's body if he finds it too uncomfortable. Similarly, she can eject his soul if she finds it too uncomfortable. But it wouldn't bode well for their relationship if they did that.

Imagine that your soul has entered your partner's body. You'll probably want to explore your temporary new home and get used to the strange sensations. But then what? Perhaps you'll go out into the world and "be" her for a while. What would that be like? Do you think you'd like it? Do you think you might like it so much that you'd want to stay inside her forever? Is there a time limit on how long your soul can stay inside her?

What if your partner feels the same way when her soul enters your body, and she wants to stay there forever? Does the system allow two people to exchange bodies permanently? And if it does, and you swap bodies, would you still want to marry the other person?

On the other hand, what if you find out a few uncomfortable truths while your soul is inside her? Perhaps you realize she has doubts about the marriage. Maybe you discover she has strong feelings for someone else. And what about her work? Is it everything she claimed it was? Are there other issues and complications that she's never mentioned? What if she won't let your soul inside her in case you find out about these things? Would you still want to marry her?

What if your soul gets trapped inside her? There might be two souls in one body – and one body without a soul, which is the definition of a zombie.

You could take this story in all sorts of directions. In fact, you could continue to write about this couple for the rest of your writing career and never exhaust all the possibilities.

123. Bonus idea

Check out the book *Humans are not from Earth* by Dr. Ellis Silver. It's packed with ideas you could turn into science fiction stories. Some are pretty mind-blowing. It also includes over 100 pages of references, on a wide range of topics, that will give you tons of ideas.

Kindle version: http://mybook.to/hanfe2k
Paperback: http://mybook.to/hanfe2p

About the Author

Dave Haslett won his first writing competition at the age of seven. The prize was a Spirograph art set, which he loved, even though he wasn't very good at it.

He then set up his own home aquarium. Not having much money, and finding the books on the subject at his local library somewhat lacking, he set about writing his own hand-illustrated encyclopedia of freshwater tropical fish. It took him nearly two years to complete, and he finished it when he was thirteen. It still looks impressive forty years later.

Always an avid reader, he was delighted when the county library service launched a contest based on the number of books people read. (You had to answer questions to prove you'd read them.) He became the first in the county to reach the target, and was presented with a shield and a certificate by a famous athlete he'd never heard of – although his mother seemed rather impressed. He was also featured in the local newspaper – the first of many appearances. They said he preferred books to TV. But that wasn't the case at all – they never even asked him about that!

An unfortunate side-effect of reading so many books in such a short time was that he'd exhausted the library's stock. They had nothing worth reading that he hadn't read already. He began cycling four miles to the next one, but it was only a little library, and he'd soon exhausted their stock too. So what now? Start writing his own, of course!

Blessed with far more ideas than he could ever use, even in several lifetimes, he launched the ideas4writers website in 2002, so he could share them with those who needed them. He soon amassed a collection of well over 5,000 ideas. He has now repackaged these into a series of books, each devoted to a single genre or topic. And you're reading one of them right now! If you thought it was good, please do him a favor and leave a review on Amazon - thanks!

The ideas4writers website is still active, but it now focuses on author services, including editing, proofreading, ghostwriting, audio transcriptions, book layouts and formatting, cover design and writing workshops.

If you're in need of any of these, please take a look at www.ideas4writers.co.uk or email dave@ideas4writers.co.uk

Made in the USA
Columbia, SC
29 January 2019